PRAISE FOR

We're All Freaking Out
(and Why We Don't Need To)

"David's words are like a much-needed road map in a time of deep confusion, fog, and anxiety. I'm thankful for David being the guide we need."

—JEFFERSON BETHKE, *New York Times* bestselling author of
Take Back Your Family

"These pages will feel like a lifeline for the anxious, overwhelmed, and burned out. David is one of the greatest shepherds of people I know, and this book is timely as we rebuild our lives."

—JENNIE ALLEN, *New York Times* bestselling author of
Get Out of Your Head and founder and visionary of IF:Gathering

"David is deeply acquainted with the greatest needs and struggles of the next generation. Prepare to be challenged and then comforted while laughing along the way."

—TIMOTHY ATEEK, executive director of Breakaway Ministries

"I have personally benefitted from David's wisdom as it relates to anxiety. If you suffer from worry, anxiety, panic attacks, or freaking out, he will be an expert guide to the peace and calm that can only be found in Jesus."

—JONATHAN POKLUDA, pastor and bestselling author of
Welcome to Adulting and *Outdated*

"David pairs lighthearted relatability with profound biblical wisdom to offer a practical guide for alleviating the anxiety that plagues us. *We're All Freaking Out* is an invaluable tool to help stop toxic thoughts before they send us into a spiral of despair."

—ALLIE BETH STUCKEY, author of
You're Not Enough (and That's Okay) and host of *Relatable*

"This book provides a timely, needed, and practical strategy for each of us to face the current epidemic of anxiety head on."

—BRAD LOMENICK, past president of Catalyst and author of
H3 Leadership and *The Catalyst Leader*

"*We're All Freaking Out* is a masterpiece—art for your soul. Through compelling stories and helpful tips, you will be encouraged and equipped to rest your worries with our God."

—JARED C. WILSON, bestselling author of
The Imperfect Disciple and *Love Me Anyway*

"In this book, David Marvin is hilariously funny and yet deadly serious. If you find yourself freaking out (which is all of us), this book shows you why you don't need to."

—KYLE IDLEMAN, bestselling author of
Not a Fan and *One at a Time*

"*We're All Freaking Out* is an outstanding book that points your anxieties back to Scripture. This is a must-read for anyone navigating the struggles in wanting to break free from anxious thoughts."

—JOE WHITE, CEO of Kanakuk Kamps

"Anxiety and worry are two of the most common reasons people come to our counseling practice. David Marvin has done a wonderful job describing what fear looks like, why it develops, and how we can tackle it by resting in Truth."

—DR. STEVEN K. LYTLE, licensed psychologist and
founding partner of Sparrow House Counseling

"In a world full of distractions where priorities, passions, and pursuits can be driven out of the brokenness in our lives, David reminds us that success and fulfillment can be found in this life if you know where to look."

—SHANE EVERETT, Shane & Shane

"One might consider that a pastor teaching on anxiety is suspect, but rest assured, David Marvin's better half is a Christian counselor. She has aptly influenced his counsel for you."

—CALEB KALTENBACH, bestselling author of
Messy Grace and *Messy Truth*

"No one can talk you out of anxiety, but some may so clearly depict the natural angst of life that we can navigate it more surely. David Marvin does just that. As a man in ministry who works with people and their struggles, David hits the nail on the head."

—TOMMY NELSON, senior pastor of Denton Bible Church

"I have watched David counsel and pastor young adults for more than a decade, and this book is only another way he will help more young people live a life of freedom."

—SHANE BARNARD, singer in the award-winning worship duo
Shane & Shane, worship leader at Watermark Community
Church, and cofounder of the Worship Initiative

"David Marvin possesses wisdom, clarity, and a keen insight into the lives of the young professionals he serves. You will be well served by this incredible resource."

—BEN STUART, pastor of Passion City Church DC,
author of *Single, Dating, Engaged, Married*

We're All Freaking Out

(and Why We Don't Need To)

We're All Freaking Out

(and Why We Don't Need To)

Finding Freedom from Your
Anxious Thoughts and Feelings

David Marvin

WATERBROOK

WE'RE ALL FREAKING OUT (AND WHY WE DON'T NEED TO)

All Scripture quotations, unless otherwise indicated, are taken from the Holy Bible, New International Version®, NIV®. Copyright © 1973, 1978, 1984, 2011 by Biblica Inc.™ Used by permission of Zondervan. All rights reserved worldwide. (www.zondervan.com). The "NIV" and "New International Version" are trademarks registered in the United States Patent and Trademark Office by Biblica Inc.™ Scripture quotations marked (ESV) are taken from the ESV® Bible (The Holy Bible, English Standard Version®), copyright © 2001 by Crossway, a publishing ministry of Good News Publishers. Used by permission. All rights reserved. Scripture quotations marked (NASB) are taken from the New American Standard Bible®, copyright © 1960, 1962, 1963, 1968, 1971, 1972, 1973, 1975, 1977, 1995 by the Lockman Foundation. Used by permission. (www.Lockman.org). Scripture quotations marked (NLT) are taken from the Holy Bible, New Living Translation, copyright © 1996, 2004, 2015 by Tyndale House Foundation. Used by permission of Tyndale House Publishers, a division of Tyndale House Ministries, Carol Stream, Illinois 60188. All rights reserved.

Italics in Scripture quotations reflect the author's added emphasis.

Details in some anecdotes and stories have been changed to protect the identities of the persons involved.

Published in the United States by WaterBrook, an imprint of Random House, a division of Penguin Random House LLC.

WATERBROOK® and its deer colophon are registered trademarks of Penguin Random House LLC.

LIBRARY OF CONGRESS CATALOGING-IN-PUBLICATION DATA
Names: Marvin, David James, author.
Title: We're all freaking out (and why we don't need to) : finding freedom from your anxious thoughts and feelings / David James Marvin.
Description: Colorado Springs : WaterBrook, 2021. |
Includes bibliographical references.
Identifiers: LCCN 2021005732 | ISBN 9780593193631 (trade paperback) |
ISBN 9780593193648 (ebook)
Subjects: LCSH: Anxiety—Religious aspects—Christianity.
Classification: LCC BV4908.5 .M339 2021 | DDC 248.8/6—dc23
LC record available at https://lccn.loc.gov/2021005732

Printed in the United States of America on acid-free paper

waterbrookmultnomah.com

9 8 7 6 5 4 3 2 1

First Edition

SPECIAL SALES
Most WaterBrook books are available at special quantity discounts when purchased in bulk by corporations, organizations, and special-interest groups. Custom imprinting or excerpting can also be done to fit special needs. For information, please email specialmarketscms@penguinrandomhouse.com.

To the one who always points me to Jesus when I'm freaking out,
who transformed how I think about anxiety,
and who is the love of my life: Calli Rae Marvin.

Contents

Part III: The Freaking Cherries On Top

Part IV: Where We Freak Out

Introduction

We're All Freaking Out

I was only a day into being married and I was freaking out. Our wedding had gone off without a hitch: my wife looked beautiful, vows were made, family and friends celebrated with us at the reception, and everything was amazing.

But waking up the next morning beside my new wife, there was something I didn't expect to be there: anxiety. A lot of it. Not anxiety about whether I'd made a mistake getting married or regarding whom I married. Those I had no concerns over. I was panicking about something entirely different: the honeymoon.

The honeymoon was my primary contribution to our wedding planning, and I had made sure the place I chose would not disappoint. So I broke the bank to set up the best honeymoon possible.

I booked us eight days at a secluded boutique-style beach resort out of the country, where pampering and luxury were guaranteed: couples massages on the beach, a sunset cruise on a yacht, rose petals in the bathtub each night, a twelve-hundred-square-foot room with our own private pool, and service to the nines. We were going to a hotel that prized itself on seclusion, quiet, and relaxation.

We were hours from experiencing all this lavishness, and what flooded my mind wasn't excitement; it was panic. *Why?*

Well, I am what people would call an extra extrovert. Being alone is not a perk to me. In the words of Ariel from Disney's *The Little Mermaid*, "I want to be where the people are."[1] I'm also someone who doesn't relax well and, honestly, doesn't really like to try to. I don't even enjoy massages. I like adventure and having things to do, and I hate being bored.

As I lay beside my beautiful new wife, I realized I had booked us a honeymoon at my own worst nightmare. *What the heck are we going to do for eight whole days?* kept playing in my mind.

So I did what you do when you're anxious: I reached for something to give me a sense of control. The next morning, I went to a local bookstore and bought twelve books. *Twelve books!* In hindsight, I am not sure why. Maybe I thought, *I'll just make this an educational trip.* I also downloaded movies and TV shows to my computer. I called my cell phone carrier and purchased an international data plan for my phone. I tried to plan and schedule things to accomplish while on the beach.

None of which helped.

My new wife could soon tell there was something on my mind. When she asked me what was wrong, I told her I thought I was having a panic attack.

But I still couldn't stop thinking, *What the heck are we going to do for eight days on the beach?* Not exactly the conversation a girl dreams of having with her new husband.

The trip came and those eight days were some of the most incredible of my life. To this day, my wife and I talk about how amazing our honeymoon was. We also look back and laugh at how crazy it was for me to be so anxious. It was my *honeymoon*, for goodness' sake.

The truth is, being anxious about a honeymoon is crazy—not just because it was a *honeymoon*, but because anxiety is always irrational. Let me explain before you write me off or think I'm insulting you.

Being anxious is normal and understandable, *but it's not rational.*

Freaking out about the future doesn't change the future; it just makes you more miserable in the present. That is why I say it's not rational. Think about it. Dwelling on anxious thoughts is not helpful to ourselves, those around us, or our circumstances. It adds nothing and only takes away. Why would we keep doing this?

Ironically, being told or even believing that being anxious doesn't help does nothing to help us not be anxious. We are anxious not because we believe it helps but because *we don't know how not to be.*

Anxiety Beyond Understanding?

People saying, "Don't be anxious," when we are anxious is like saying, "Just fall asleep," to someone struggling to fall asleep at night. It doesn't help. If we could just stop, we would.

But the Bible promises that we can experience a peace that "surpasses all understanding" (Philippians 4:7, ESV)—a peace greater than our ability to explain or put into words. If that is promised, why do we rarely feel that peace? For most of us, the opposite is true: we experience *anxiety* that goes beyond understanding.

We get stuck in moments, or even seasons, of crippling fear and worry that we can't explain and find hard to express to others. We experience anxious feelings that paralyze us, keep us from sleeping, rob us of our ability to be present with friends, and just suck the life out of us.

Scripture also refers to God keeping in perfect peace those who look to him (see Isaiah 26:3, NLT). We think, *Really? In perfect peace? Is that even possible?* It doesn't seem so. Not many people I know live in perfect peace. For most of us, it's an imperfect peace, at best. More often our experience is closer to "in constant fear" or "with alarming anxiousness" or "weighed down by worry" or "so nervous I have no nails left to bite."

But as we will see, for believers in Christ, this doesn't have to be the case for much, if not all, of our anxiety. I don't say Christians can always be free from all anxiety at all times, because that is often not the case. Anxiety forms as a result of one or more of three underlying types of reasons: physiological, psychological, and spiritual. While most often the causes are psychological and spiritual, there are times when something physiological is going on. When someone says, "I have anxiety," it's like someone saying, "I have a problem with my computer." In the case of the computer, there's a problem with either the software (maybe a software update is needed or there's a virus) or the hardware (the physical components, like the keyboard).

When it comes to dealing with anxiety, there are times the problem is spiritual or psychological (our "software"), and other times when something physiological (our "hardware") is going on—for example, a hormonal imbalance or serotonin deficiency. In these pages, we will explore God's plan for dealing with the spiritual and psychological factors behind our anxiety. If the root cause of your anxiety is physiological, you can still learn plenty from this book, yet I encourage you to seek a qualified medical doctor to fully attend to your situation. And although I touch on the topic of medication in the FAQ section, I recommend consulting with a physician, therapist, or other qualified individual before deciding if it's right for you.

Thankfully, for most of us, the bulk of our anxiety issues involves our psychology (personality and experiences) and spiritual life (walking in relationship with God in a sinful world). So that will be our focus in this book.

What's in a Name?

One of the biggest challenges of writing this particular book is the different meanings people have associated with words like *anxiety, fear,* and *worry.* Then throw in terms like *nervousness, panic attack,* and *anxiety disorder* (not to mention *losing it, freaking out,* and *flipping out*), and the waters get even muddier.

The word translated in the Bible as "being worried" is also translated as "being anxious." So, while the Bible does not distinguish between being worried and being anxious, that does not mean there is no such thing as clinical anxiety or generalized anxiety disorders. I discuss both and more in the FAQ section.

But the word the Bible uses most often for anxiety, worry, and anxiousness is the Greek term *merimnao,* which means "dwelling on or pondering fearful or anxious thoughts." According to pastor and professor Bill Klein, "In ancient Greek literature, it is used to convey the concept of meditation."[2]

When the Bible says, "Do not be anxious" in Philippians 4:6, it is *not* saying, "Don't have anxious thoughts." That's impossible. We can't just *not have* those thoughts. Rather, it's saying, "Do not *meditate* or *dwell* on those anxious thoughts." That *is* possible; we *can* choose not to continue ruminating on anxious thoughts. Think of it like this: you may not be able to stop some burglar from bursting into your house, but you can choose not to invite him to sit down and stay awhile.

Do not meditate on anxious thoughts. Who would disagree with that? I'm sure you've never heard someone say, "Here's what really helped turn my life around: I began every morning meditating on fear, trying to play out every anxious thought about what could happen that day. It fixed all my problems!" No, that's nuts.

So, the definition I'll use for being worried and anxious is "dwelling on anxious and fearful feelings and thoughts about future or potential problems."

The Struggle Is Real

If you've struggled with anxiety, fear, or worry, you are not alone. If you haven't, you don't live on Planet Earth and I'm not sure how you got hold of this book. The truth is, everyone gets anxious. I think I can go a step further and say that everyone has moments better described as "freaking out"—those times when panic, fear, worry, or anxiety overwhelms us. It's part of life for most of us, and a *way of life* for some of us.

According to the Anxiety and Depression Association of America, anxiety disorders have reached epidemic levels, affecting forty million adults age eighteen and older just in the United States alone.[3]

In fact, in 2019, the American Psychiatric Association found that two in three Americans said they were anxious, and "nearly one in three adults (32%) say they are more anxious than they were last year."[4] That means for *most* of us, the struggle is real. And research shows that younger adults are more anxious than older ones. "About 70% of adults 18 to 34 years are somewhat or extremely anxious about paying bills or keeping their family safe."[5] In fact, millennials and Generation Z have the highest levels of anxiety.[6]

Adults today are between two and three times more likely than people of previous generations to experience depression,[7] which is often caused by prolonged anxiety. Overdose deaths for medications such as Xanax, Librium, Valium, and Ativan—which are commonly prescribed to treat anxiety, phobias, panic attacks, insomnia, and more—have quadrupled in the past twenty years, according to the National Institute on Drug Abuse.[8] And this was *before* the onset of the COVID-19 pandemic, which caused even more anxiety, more panic attacks, and a sharp increase in the use of anti-anxiety medication.[9]

It's Getting Worse

It doesn't seem like anxiety is going away anytime soon. It actually appears to be getting worse and influencing us earlier in life. One study found that "the average high school kid today has the same level of anxiety as the average psychiatric patient in the early 1950's."[10] That's crazy! Or maybe, according to people who lived in that decade, *we* are crazy.

Why is the problem growing worse? There are many potential reasons, but one is the rapid cultural transformation of recent decades. Some researchers suggest that the Western world's "environment and social order have changed more in the last thirty years than they have in the previous three hundred."[11] And that research was published in 2010! Before Instagram, iPads, Amazon's Alexa, Netflix originals, Uber, DoorDash, and more have further transformed our world. It's no wonder people are freaking out: change is stressful!

The explosion in popularity of smartphones is a clear example. These devices changed much more than how we talk on the phone. They are portable computers that constantly bombard us with massive amounts of information, some of which is helpful, some interesting, and some a total waste of time (like those cat videos your aunt sends).

Think about how much we have flooding our attention, thanks to smartphones, that no one in history previously had the blessing or burden of carrying. If there is something to get anxious over, that little computer in your pocket is *it*. Want to worry about threats of pandemics, global warming, terrorist attacks, mounting national debt, foreign dictatorships, and more? Just set a news alert. Need more relational drama in your life? There's an app for that. Download and turn on notifications to get the latest intel on pop-culture drama, such as which celebrity is breaking up with which other celebrity.

On top of that, social media provides access to a world of distraction, discontentment, and maybe even depression. From tweets fueling the latest-trending controversy to Instagram posts feeding envy—not to mention the never-ending barrage of emails and text messages—it's surprising we can ever get a break.

Life seems to be moving faster than ever, and it's virtually impossible to catch our breath. When we stop and think about it, the enormous spikes in anxiety make total sense.

Young and Anxious

Anxiety can be a part of our lives regardless of our age, but it is now especially prevalent in the young-adult years, between ages eighteen and thirty-five. It's a unique time because we must make decisions that dramatically shape the direction of our lives. That means pressure! One study found that "80% of life's most significant events take place by about age 35."[12]

In young adulthood, you are often deciding whom to marry, what career path to take, and so many other things that affect your future, all without clear guidelines on how to make those life-altering decisions.

This is dramatically different from our lives as kids. Remember when the biggest decisions you had to make were which Lunchables to take to school and whether you should listen to Spotify or Apple Music? Life used to be so simple.

Up until young adulthood, there are pretty clear tracks to run on: When you finish elementary school, you go to middle school. When you finish middle school, you go to high school. When you finish high school, you go to college. In college, there's freshman year, then sophomore year, then junior year, then senior year, then sometimes another senior year for a victory lap. But after that, it's as if the tracks run out right as you approach a bridge. And life can feel like the derailed train free-falling through the air:

- *Am I in the right career?*
- *Is this person "the one"?*
- *Where am I going to live?*
- *How am I going to pay off my student loans?*
- *How am I going to afford health insurance?*

An endless number of uncertainties arise.

On top of that, many young adults are walking through these years alone. Over the past forty years, the average age of first-time marriage has gone from twenty-four to thirty for men and from twenty-two to twenty-eight for women.[13] Previously, young adults were at least walking through this time in their lives with a spouse, but these days they are more likely to be single during these defining decision-making years.

Yes, we have numerous tools at hand for digital connection to family, friends, and coworkers, but truly meaningful relationships aren't quite as common. In fact, only one in three young adults (ages eighteen to thirty-five) "often feel deeply cared for by those around them (33%) or that someone believes in them (32%)."[14]

The uncertainty of life and the loneliness of facing it on our own typically heighten anxiety. The young-adult life stage is basically a natural period for anxiousness, fear, and worry. But as we will see, it doesn't have to be.

There, I Said It

Tragically, the church has often failed in helpfully addressing the issue of anxiety, with such ineffective banalities as "If you just had more faith, you would not be anxious" or similar platitudes that only cause the anxious person to feel shame on top of his or her feelings of anxiety. Think about how ridiculous this is. When was the last (or first) time you heard someone say, "You know what cured my anxiety? Shame"? Yeah, *never.*

There is more to the battle of anxiety than just having more faith. In fact, some of the *godliest* people I know *struggle with anxiety* currently or have in the past, and some of the *least anxious* people are the most *ungodly.* Simply suggesting that people with anxiety just ramp up their faith is not only unhelpful but also insulting.

That is *not* to say that we shouldn't be pointing people to God's Word for help and guidance as a first line of defense. There is life-changing wisdom, comfort, and guidance in the Bible that should be offered to those who struggle. We'll talk about this in greater detail throughout the book.

Yet often our reaction when someone struggles with anxiety is to immediately push him or her to see a counselor or psychiatrist outside the church for help. Don't get me wrong; those are wonderful professions and are appropriate and even necessary at times. Don't believe me? I am married to a licensed professional counselor who has for the past decade worked primarily with young adults who struggle with anxiety. If I didn't support counseling, things would be pretty awkward at home.

The counseling profession is important. I have personally gone to counseling and found it incredibly helpful. But as my wife and thousands of counselors would agree, God's Word should be our first line of defense against anxiety. Taking the step to see a counselor should not exclude putting into practice the principles God gives us for dealing with anxiety, fear, panic, and worry. Professional counseling is a good supplement to God's Word, but it is not a replacement.

Yeah . . . That's Not What the Bible Says

Why do people ignore what the Bible says about anxiety? In my experience, it is almost always because they misunderstand what the Bible teaches as it relates to anxiety, which leads them to see its teachings as irrelevant and outdated on this topic.

If you were to ask the average Christian, "What does the Bible teach about anxiety and worry?" my guess is you would get answers like, "It says to stop" or "It says don't worry; just pray" or "Don't be anxious; you just need to trust God."

All those statements are . . . well . . . kind of true, but not entirely.

The teachings throughout Scripture are far more helpful and practical than simply "Stop being anxious." Like I said, telling people to just stop being anxious doesn't work. If they could "just stop," they would have already.

The Bible gives us real tools that can truly help us fight anxiety, fear, and worry. God gave us these tools thousands of years ago, and—as we'll learn—science and psychology are still catching up.

In the chapters ahead, we will explore what the Bible actually teaches and how to put the principles into practice in a way that allows us to experience real peace.

How does that sound? Pretty good, right? I truly believe our lives will be transformed as we learn what God has to say about anxiety and how to apply his truth to our lives.

What This Book *Is Not*

Before moving forward, let me make clear what this book is *not*.

This book is not a substitute for counseling, nor is it a one-stop shop to immediately fix every anxiety disorder, every panic disorder, every post-traumatic stress disorder, and every expression of anxiety.

This book is definitely *not* to shame people who have anxiety. Christians who are able to better control their anxious thoughts can sometimes make those of us who struggle with anxiety ashamed and even more anxious. I promise you won't get that here.

This book is *not* anti-psychology. Psychology is not God, but when applied and practiced correctly, it *is* a gift from God. Like all medical fields can inform us about various aspects of our physical bodies, psychology gives us greater glimpses into how our minds work and how to retrain our thinking and thus change our feelings.

What This Book *Is*

Over the past ten years, I have worked as a pastor at the Porch, a young-adult ministry in Dallas, Texas, that brings in thousands of people every week to worship, with many more joining us via satellite locations around America. This role has allowed me to work directly with tens of thousands of young men and women. I have seen up close the dramatic spike in anxiety, panic attacks, and worry and what effect those are having on their lives. Many of these young adults were raised in church and became Christians at a young age but never understood what the Bible teaches or how to put what it says into practice.

As a result of what I was observing, I began to prioritize teaching principles from the Bible to provide a strategy for what to do when anxiety strikes. Consider this book that strategy. We will walk through how to identify your anxiety and what is fueling it. Then we will examine the tools God offers to help us experience peace, learning exactly how to use them in our lives. We will also explore the most common areas that are sources of anxiety among young adults: romantic anxiety, career anxiety, financial anxiety, and personal anxiety (a.k.a. insecurity anxiety).

You are about to discover why *you* don't have to freak out, even if everyone else is.

The Bible's Most Repeated Command

God's Word has a lot to say about fear, anxiety, and worry. In fact, the most repeated command in all of Scripture is "Fear not." Think about that. God tells us not to fear more than he tells us not to murder, commit adultery, or steal. God tells us not to fear more than he tells us to pray or love our neighbor. At least 366 times, we are commanded in the Bible not to give way to fear. That is once for every day of the year, even on a leap year. It is clear God does not want us to experience lives owned by fear.

None of us wants to live imprisoned by fear, anxiety, and worry. I have met with thousands of people, and never once have I heard someone say, "I am willing to give God all of my life, just not my anxiety. That I want to keep and enjoy for myself." I may not know you personally, but I'm certain that if there were an "eliminate anxiety" button, you would push it.

The problem is not that we are unwilling to let go of our anxiety; it's that we don't know how. In this book, we're going to discover how. Hope will come as you keep turning the pages.

God loves you and doesn't want you to be ruled by anxiety and fear. He invites all of us into lives marked by his peace instead of our panic and tells us how to get there.

Are you ready to begin?

Part I

Why We Freak Out

1

The Fog of Fear

Identifying the Reasons We're Anxious

I have yard envy. I had to confess before we continue. Yes, I know I sound like the grumpy old guy who yells, "Stay off my lawn!" at little kids, but hear me out. I live next door to a family that should win an award for how well they keep their lawn. It's always lush and full. I would be lying if I said I hadn't entertained doing a picnic over there.

My lawn, on the other hand, is patchy with lots of spots where the grass has died, even though it gets plenty of water. The problem is that it's full of weeds. My yard looks like a bald dude who's using Rogaine to try to grow hair but it's coming in kind of wild and irregular in a few random spots around his head. I don't know why, but I am *amazing* at growing weeds but *awful* at growing grass.

Every spring is another season of trying to remove weeds and grow grass. Years of doing this has given me a bad back and a PhD in weed removal. I've learned that if you don't remove the weeds, they will choke out the grass around them. They quite literally suck the life out of your lawn. And unless you pull the weeds out by their roots, you *still* have weeds. You think you've removed them, but they have *not* gone away and will keep growing.

Sometimes when I'm out in my yard—crying, or lying defeated in a dirt patch, or thinking about how if I torched my neighbor's yard mine wouldn't look so bad anymore—I realize those weeds are a picture of the anxiety and worry in our lives. If we don't deal with them, they choke the life out of us. In fact, the origin of the word *worry* in English comes from an old German word meaning "to strangle or choke." Worry and anxiety strangle us mentally, emotionally, spiritually, and even physically.

Also, like weeds, if anxiety is not addressed at its roots, it isn't going away. We might think we've removed it, but then we'll discover we haven't, and it will continue choking the life out of us. The roots of the weeds in our lawn are underground. And, like weeds, the roots of our anxiety are also beneath the surface . . . of our minds and hearts.

Good news: it is possible to remove weeds in your lawn, and it is possible to remove the anxious feelings in your heart. Like getting rid of weeds, it's not easy, but you can do it.

Jedi Jesus

What do you think Jesus preached about when he gave a sermon? Remember, it was two thousand years ago, so he probably wasn't warning of the dangers of dating apps, Zoom fatigue, or Netflix and chilling.

We have some of Jesus's preaching recorded in the Bible, including his most famous talk, called the Sermon on the Mount, because he delivers it from a mountainside.

In this teaching, Jesus addresses the topic of . . . anxiety. Imagine that. I guess people have been anxious for a long time!

In the chapters ahead, we will explore more of Jesus's teaching on anxiety. For now, I want to focus on a few penetrating questions he asks his audience in the Sermon on the Mount. I think we'll find they are still relevant to our anxiety today.

Jesus says,

> I tell you, do not worry about your life, what you will eat or drink; or about your body, what you will wear. (Matthew 6:25)

Jesus covers what his audience would have worried about: food and clothing.

In that day, there wasn't a local grocery store or a fridge full of food. Chick-fil-A was not open on Sundays, and . . . well, it was *never* open back then. Restaurants didn't exist. You got up every morning hoping you'd have enough to eat that day.

There also wasn't mass production of clothing. Most folks had one or two outfits total. They couldn't go buy a new outfit at the mall, because there were no malls! Anxiety about "What if we run out of food?" or "What if our clothes wear out and we can't afford to replace them?" was real.

But Jesus says, "Don't worry about that." Whatever you are stressed about, he would tell you not to spend time worrying about it. More on why ahead, but let's take a look at a genius question he asks next:

> Is not life more than food, and the body more than clothes?

Let me pause before going on. Why do you think Jesus asks that question? Is he looking for an answer or being rhetorical? Since he is Jesus—and, you know, *God*—it's safe to assume he knows the answer. Jesus wants to force his audience to put the objects of their worries into a bigger perspective. He was the original Jedi-mind-trick master.

He is basically saying, *Hey, guys, does food equal life? That's all life is about? If you had all the food you needed for the rest of your days, would that be like the best thing ever? Really? Is the point of life really acquiring food?*

His audience would have known, *Of course food doesn't equal life. Food is important, but life is not equal to just food.*

This leads Jesus to ask the logical question of *Then why would you spend so much of your life worried about it?*

Remember, the Bible's definition of worrying or being anxious is not "to have an occasional anxious thought"; it's to dwell on our anxious thoughts. Jesus is saying, *If there is more to life than food and clothes, why would you give so much of your life to being anxious about them?*

It's his attempt to pull the people back so they can better see the objects of their anxiety. When we are anxious, we get so nearsighted that it's difficult for us to see anything other than the thing we are anxious about.

One reason is because anxiety is amazing at taking something small and inflating it to enormous proportions. Jesus is helping his audience deflate the power of their worries by putting them into perspective.

Fog Machine of Fear

I read once that a dense fog large enough to cover seven city blocks a hundred feet deep is made up of just one glass of water expanded into millions and millions of droplets. *Whaaaaa?* Something so small can expand into something so big.

In the same way, the object of our anxiety is always smaller than the size it grows to in our thoughts. Anxiety operates in our minds like a fog machine with a glass of water, expanding and stretching our fear-filled thoughts as far as we will allow it.

A thought so small like *I am not sure where I am going to live after my roommate moves out* enters the "fog machine of fear" in our minds and gets stretched way out of proportion, with us ending up in a panic. That simple idea can stretch into something like this:

> I am not sure where I am going to live after my roommate moves out. I need to find a roommate to pay half the rent or I can't afford to live here and I'll be kicked to the curb. I don't know anyone looking for a place to live. Maybe I should post something on Craigslist or Facebook to find someone. Great, then I'll end up with a psychopath who murders me in my sleep. Oh no, my op-

tions are homelessness or being murdered! Either
way, my life is over.

Without trying, we end up in a "fog of fear" of our own making. It's paralyzing and miserable. But remember, enormous fog comes from a *small* amount of water. What if we could see our anxiety as a glass of water rather than the giant fog? Dealing with it would become *much* easier. The good news is, you *can*. Let's figure out how.

Anxious for Something

If you are wrestling with anxiety and go see a counselor, he or she will often do what Jesus did. To deflate the power your anxiety is having over you, the counselor will ask you questions that will reveal what you are *actually anxious* about.

Like I said, I am married to a counselor—maybe because God knew I would need round-the-clock therapy, not just occasional help. My wife works primarily with young adults who struggle with anxiety. She (and other therapists) will often do something like the following. (Side note: I am about to give you, for free, what would cost $120 an hour from a counselor. You're welcome.)

Suppose someone were seeing a counselor. Let's call him Kyle. Kyle brings up that he is anxious about some layoffs his company is going through. Here's how the counselor might try to help him get to the bottom of his fears.

KYLE: My company is downsizing and laying off staff. I am anxious that I may lose my job.

COUNSELOR: Well, what happens if you get laid off?

KYLE: I'd have to find a job quickly or I won't be able to pay my rent.

COUNSELOR: What happens if you can't afford to pay your rent?

KYLE: I'd have to move back in with my parents.

> COUNSELOR: What happens if you have to move back in
> with your parents?
>
> KYLE: I'd feel so embarrassed, like I was a failure.

Let me hit pause in this made-up dialogue. (It's my story, so I can pause when I want to.)

What Kyle thinks he is anxious about is losing his job. What he is *actually* anxious about is moving in with his parents and being *seen as a failure.* Of course, moving in with one's parents is *not* the definition of failure. But my point is, he is actually anxious about what people think of him. If he is going to *not* be anxious, he needs to know why he is anxious in the first place.

In order to combat your anxiety, you need to ask yourself, *What am I anxious about, really?* Will that make the problem go away? No. But it will at least let you see what you are actually afraid of. My guess is that it will deflate your anxiety by allowing you to see your fears for what they really are.

More importantly, it's also the first step to dealing with your anxiety.

You Are Here

I don't like going to the mall. It stresses me out. I feel like I can't breathe. I don't know where the stores are, I struggle to find my way out, and I continually have to fight the temptation to go crouch in the fetal position in some abandoned corner eating an Auntie Anne's pretzel.

To prevent that soul-sucking mall experience, I have mastered the art of online shopping. You'd be amazed at my ability to order everything online just so I don't have to go to the store. Except for one store: the Apple store. Yes, I am an Apple-product guy. (If you are an Android user, know that I am praying for you.)

About once a year, some Apple product of mine needs to be fixed or I find out about some new Apple product I "need," so I head to the mall. I park, go inside, and begin my *Maze Runner* experience. I start walking through the intricate labyrinth, only to realize I've done it again: I've parked on the completely wrong side of the mall. I begin to think the people who run the mall move the Apple store every few months. (Or I just have no sense of direction and hate malls.)

Because I don't know my way around, I always look for the sign that has the map telling you where everything is. It's like the last physical map left in society. Something about it makes me feel like I am hunting for buried treasure.

When I read the map, I look for two things: Where is the Apple store, and where am I? You know that little star that says, "You are here"? I love that little star! Because in order for me to get to where I want to be, I need to know where I am. Without that little star, the map is useless.

The same is true in our journey to be free (or at least freer) from anxiety. We have to know where we are. We need to admit we are anxious.

Too many of us feel shame over our anxiety and try to pretend it isn't there. That doesn't help. It can actually make us *more* anxious. (Now we're not just anxious; we're also anxious that we're anxious!) And pretending we are not anxious when we are does not mean we are more spiritual; it means we are in denial.

Don't be ashamed of anxious feelings. You cannot change what you will not face. So, *why* are you anxious? What are you worried about? What keeps you awake at night? What are you afraid of?

The First Step

We are going to develop a plan for what to do once we identify our anxieties, but for now I just want you to be honest with yourself by admitting what you are feeling. Write it out or say it out loud to yourself. The next time you are anxious, chase down your anxiety and face what's beneath it by filling in these blanks: *I am anxious about* _____ *because* _____. Maybe for you it's one of the following:

- *I am anxious about being single the rest of my life because I am scared to die alone.* (That took a morbid turn.)
- *I am anxious about saying the wrong thing at work because I am afraid of what people may think of me.*
- *I am anxious about getting married because I don't want to end up divorced.*
- *I am anxious about my student loans because they might prevent me from buying a home.*
- *I am anxious that my neighbor's lawn looks like it belongs to some European castle, while mine looks like an abandoned gopher compound, because I'm afraid people will think I'm a loser.*

See how it works? Now it's your turn:

I am anxious about _____ because _____.

What are you anxious about, *really*? If you are going to allow it to choke the life out of you, you should at least find out what it is. If you deny or dismiss your anxiety, you will eventually be dominated by it. It's time to face it by first embracing it.

What Will You Choose to Grow?

Here is something you probably know but have never really thought about. Grass and weeds require the same soil to grow: *dirt*. While you want grass and not weeds, which one grows really depends on you.

In the same way, fear and faith also require the same soil to grow: *uncertainty*. Without uncertainty, fear can't grow, but neither can faith. The same unknowns of the future related to your marriage, job, health, family, and finances provide just as much an opportunity to grow your faith as to grow your fear. Just like with weeds and grass, when it comes to faith and fear, what you grow in the long run depends on you.

If you will begin to uncover the roots of your anxious feelings and then address them with truths from God's Word, your faith will grow in the very soil in which your fear is present. Why? Because addressing your anxiety with what God's Word says about your worries *is an act of faith*. Faith is like a muscle: the more you use it, the stronger it grows. The inverse is also true: the less you use it, the more it withers away.

So, can you expect to never be anxious again? No more than someone can pluck out all the weeds in their lawn and expect to never see one pop up again. Anxious feelings will likely pop up the rest of your life. You will identify them and go after their roots with God's Word. *Um, sounds great, but how, specifically?* Glad you asked. That's exactly what we're going to cover next!

2

"Check Engine" Lights
The Truth About Anxious Feelings

Our family often goes to Costco on Saturdays. Because we have little kids, we are constantly looking for inexpensive fun things to do. We have low standards, and Costco—with its free samples and enormous inventory of things you didn't realize you needed till you saw them—meets our requirements. So, one Saturday not long ago, I loaded the kids into my wife's SUV, and I jumped in to drive her car, with the plan to meet up at Costco.

I quickly noticed her "check engine" light was on. I called her and said, "Your 'check engine' light is on. Do you know that?"

She responded, "Oh yeah. It's been on for a while."

"A while?" I replied, shocked. I could not believe she had been driving around—*for a while!*—with her car screaming as loud as it was capable, "You have something to address in here."

Now, you are likely to fall into one of two camps as it relates to the "check engine" light being illuminated. There is the camp of people I belong to. When this light appears, we immediately take the car to the closest auto-repair place and get it worked on. The other camp thinks more like my wife: *I'm sure it's nothing too bad. It's basically like I'm low on gas. I'll fix it at some point.*

Whatever camp you are in, I think we can all agree the "check engine" light is a signal that there's something about the car that needs to be taken care of. *That's why it's on.*

Negative human emotions—such as fear, anxiety, and panic—operate in the exact same way. When we feel them, they indicate something going on beneath the surface in our hearts and minds. They are signals that something needs to be addressed. In order to do so, we have to figure out what is causing the emotions. To do that, we need to understand what causes emotions and how they work.

Every time we feel the emotion of anxiety, fear, or worry, it involves an intersection of our beliefs and values.[1] We experience anxious, scared, depressed, or panicked feelings because we *believe* something we *value* is or may be threatened. To deal with those feelings, we have to understand what values and beliefs are causing them.

So here now is an Emotions 101 crash course. File this info away in "Stuff no one ever told me that helps me understand me."

Values

If we don't see something as valuable, it will not evoke an emotion. For example, when I see a squirrel running in the street, I feel nothing. I am not panicked or concerned. If you are reading this and love rodents, don't judge me. (Also, who loves rodents?)

On the other hand, when I see a *child* running in the street, I feel afraid. I would run toward the child, yelling, "Stay on the sidewalk. You don't want to get hit by a car!" Why? Because I value children more than I value squirrels.

When I see *my own* children running in the street, I am *flooded* with fear. Those emotions are stirred up because of how valuable my kids are to me. You won't have anxiety, or any other emotion, unless it involves something you value.

Feel anxious about losing your job? Maybe it's because you value making an income.

Feel anxious about your dating relationship? It's probably because you value that person or that relationship.

Feel anxious about what people think about you? It's probably because you value their opinions.

Regardless of whether your values are right, biblical, helpful, or appropriate, they *are* fueling your anxious and fearful emotions.

Beliefs

The same is true with our beliefs. Emotions like panic, worry, and anxiety are driven by something you believe. What do I mean by "something you believe"?

Let's say I see my wife walking in our front yard and she steps onto one of those rare patches of grass and I notice something I believe is a snake. I will feel fear and yell, "Watch out!" But if I believe it is a stick, not a snake, I will not feel the emotion of fear. Why? Because of what I believed.

Here's where things get interesting. We don't have to believe something is 100 percent true in order to experience the emotions of fear and anxiety. Our belief that something *could* be true is enough to send us into freak-out mode.

I mentioned watching my wife stepping onto the grass. Let's say she's walking toward what was actually a stick. If I thought it *might* be a snake, I would still feel fear and concern. When it comes to emotions, it doesn't have to be true; we just have to *believe* it might be true.

Every time we are anxious, something we believe or value is involved. To address our anxiety, we must address the specific beliefs and values at their roots. This is why someone saying, "Don't be afraid," or, "Just calm down," never works. (Don't you want to slap people when they say that? No? Just me?) Fear fades only when the root beliefs informing it are dealt with.

When you understand your emotions, you have the key to combating them.

Shape of You

Your entire life has been shaped by what you believe and value. In other words, you didn't wake up today saying, "Whoa. What happened? I believe some things. And I value some things! None of it was true yesterday, but now . . . YES!" No, you arrived at your beliefs over time. You have been shaped by your family of origin, the home you were raised in, friendships, experiences, traumatic events, and influential people in your life.

Our lives are shaped by what we believe and value *and* our emotions, because our beliefs and values drive our emotions. That explains why two people might be in the same scenario but one is anxious while the other is not. They have different reactions because they have different beliefs and value systems.

Maybe you were raised in a home where money was talked about as the ultimate source of security. You heard messages like "Honey, *what matters most* is getting a great degree and a good job that pays well." Today you can quickly get anxious when it comes to finances. Why? Because the thing that you believe is valuable, and even "matters most," is being threatened. But the anxiety you feel is rooted in a lie. For Christians, money is *not* what matters most and is not our ultimate source of security; God is.

You might believe conflict is always a bad thing. You were raised in a home where it was stressed, "We don't fight," or in a family where your parents fought a lot and it really scared you. The result is that you embrace the belief that conflict is always negative. Now anytime conflict happens in a dating relationship, you panic and think you need to break up.

See how this works? Your anxious feelings are rooted in what you believe and value. The only way to move toward freedom from those feelings is to address those beliefs and values with truth from God's Word.

Sword Drills

When I was growing up, there was a game at church we played called sword drills. It was basically a competition to see who could open their Bible and turn most quickly to the verse our Sunday school teacher called out. At the time, there were two things I didn't understand about this game. First, why did the kids with Bibles that had zippers around the outside always win? Did it have more to do with the zipper or the type of person who would have a Bible with a zipper on it? Mysteries only God knows the answer to, I guess.

The other thing I never understood then was why we called this "sword drills." There was no sword involved. Just a book. Years later, I learned that the reference comes from something the Bible says about itself and how it acts as a sword in our hearts and lives. Look at what the Bible says about this in Hebrews 4:12:

> The word of God is living and active, sharper than any two-edged sword, piercing to the division of soul and of spirit, of joints and of marrow, and discerning the thoughts and intentions [your beliefs and the things of value to you] of the heart. (ESV)

The Bible says it is like a sword or knife able to cut through what's going on in our hearts. Like a knife designed to cut through weeds at their roots, the Bible is perfectly designed to help us cut through the roots of our anxiety. When we feel anxious, God's Word can help us clarify if what we're believing is a lie or if what we're valuing isn't really that valuable.

The more we can align our beliefs and values to what the Bible teaches, the more we cut through the roots fueling our anxiety.

The Lies Beneath

The other day I was trying to talk my friend Tyler off the ledge. Tyler is in ministry, so he doesn't make a ton of money, and he was freaking out about whether he will be able to pay for his kids' college when they get older. Understandable. I've had the same feelings about my own kids. I realize you may be more anxious about your own student loans, not someday paying for your kids' college, but the same lesson applies. I think our conversation unearthed the root beliefs creating his anxiety. Allow me to illustrate the point I am making:

TYLER: Sometimes I think about how I may not be able to pay for my kids' college one day. It stresses me out!

ME: What if you can't afford to pay for your kids' college someday?

TYLER: I guess they'd have to take out a loan or get a scholarship. Maybe they won't even go to college.

ME: What if they have to take out a loan or get a scholarship, or what if they don't go to college?

TYLER: Well, then I would feel like I was a bad dad. I didn't provide in the way I should have for my kids. I'm not a good dad.

ME: Is that what God says a good dad does—pays for college? Is it possible there could be a good dad who doesn't pay for college, or there could be a bad dad who did pay for college? On the list of the top ten things that make a good dad, where would paying for college be?

TYLER: I guess that's not what God says is the definition of a good dad.

Ironically, his overwhelming fear about not being a good dad *someday* was taking away the opportunity he had to be a good dad *today*. His fear was rooted in believing the lie "All good dads pay for their kids' college." Like most lies we accept as true, this one was never something he consciously decided to believe. Lies typically creep into our psyche, and until they are exposed as lies, we don't even realize they are there.

I'm not sure what you are anxious about, but I do know that the only way you can experience increased freedom from those feelings is to chase down the roots informing them and replace any lies or wrong beliefs with the truth from God's Word.

Destination Freedom

One time Jesus said something interesting about what is required to experience freedom, whether from unhealthy behaviors or unpleasant emotions like anxiety:

> If you abide in my word, you are truly my disciples,
> and you will know the truth, and the truth will set
> you free. (John 8:31-32, ESV)

Most people think Jesus is just saying, "Read your Bible and you will experience freedom." While I am all for people reading their Bibles, that is too simplistic and misses the profound teaching he is laying out. Jesus doesn't say we should read the Bible; he says we should *abide* in it.

We don't use the word *abide* on a regular basis. It means "to remain in a state or dwell in a certain place."[2] Jesus is saying that if you will learn to live in and from God's Word, you will know the truth and step in the direction of freedom.

T-R-U-T-H

All this sounds great, but how do I actually let the truth from God's Word bring me freedom from my anxiety? Let me tell you about a tool a counselor shared with me when I was doing research for this book. It is called a truth journal and involves working through an acronym of the word *truth*. I have adapted this from the original TRUTH Model created by Dr. Chris Thurman.[3]

T	Trigger
R	Root Beliefs and Values
U	Unpleasant Emotion (anxiety, for example)
T	Truth from God's Word
H	Helpful Future Response

Here's how a person could use this tool. One day a young woman (let's call her Ashley) is scrolling through Instagram (a totally Ashley thing to do) and comes across a friend of hers from college who just got engaged. She sees pictures of the proposal with the new fiancé on one knee, of her friend showcasing the ring, and of their friends and family at an engagement party.

Rather than feeling excitement for them, Ashley is struck with anxiety because she is so single with nothing close to a prospect to mingle. She begins feeling a mixture of sadness (she's not where she wants to be relationally) and panic (*What if I am alone forever?*).

How can the truth set her free from that?

I would walk Ashley through the TRUTH tool to help her experience freedom. The middle of the tool is identifying the "Unpleasant Emotion" (U), which is Ashley's panic about being single. But what "Triggered" (T) that panic? It was "seeing someone's engagement pictures on Instagram." Often, when we try to fight our anxiety, we focus on getting rid of the triggers. In Ashley's case, that might include getting off Instagram or unfollowing everyone except single people.

While those steps may bring temporary relief, they will not bring lasting freedom from her anxiety over being single. It's impossible to avoid the million other things that could trigger anxiety about being single: a Taylor Swift song, an "Every kiss begins with Kay" commercial promoting jewelry, her family asking at the holidays if she's "met anyone," and on and on.

To remove all the triggers, she would have to go live alone in the wilderness the rest of her life. Yet living alone would *not* help her fear of *being* alone.

To experience freedom, it helps to acknowledge the triggers, but we don't need to remove them. Ashley must address the "Root Beliefs and Values" (R) that cause her to be triggered.

What is the root belief informing the anxiety? In real life, this part takes some prayerful introspection and perhaps help from trusted Christian friends. You may not get to all the root beliefs behind your anxiety all at once. That's okay. You can work through them as you identify them.

Because I made Ashley up, I am also going to make her root belief up. Ashley's root belief is "If I am single the rest of my life, my life isn't worth living."

T   Trigger: Seeing someone's engagement pictures on Instagram.

R   Root Beliefs and Values: A life of singleness is not a life worth living.

U   Unpleasant Emotion: Anxiety about singleness.

So what about "Truth" (T)? What does God's Word say about Ashley's belief that "A life of singleness is not a life worth living"? It says she is believing a lie. You can live an incredible life despite being single. In fact, Paul said he wished everyone were single (see 1 Corinthians 7:38). *Whaaaaa?* Yep. Because by "refrain[ing] from marriage," a person can "do even better" (ESV) in living a life devoted to God's kingdom. Also, if Ashley's belief about singleness were right, then Jesus's life was not one worth living.

If Ashley were a real person, there would likely be a number of beliefs informing her anxiety about singleness. She might believe she will be unable to provide for herself, that she won't have kids, or that a woman's worth is connected to her ability to have children—none of which aligns with God's Word.

God has promised to provide, and a person's value has nothing to do with the number of children they have. As Ashley reminds herself of these truths and meditates on them, she will begin to experience more freedom from her anxiety.

This brings us to the final letter in TRUTH: the "Helpful Future Response" (H). This is our "pregame strategy" for the next time these feelings rise up. In other words, once we have identified the beliefs and values that don't line up with God's Word and have confronted them with God's truth, we are ready to ask ourselves, *The next time I'm triggered and feel these emotions, what am I going to do?*

Ashley decides that the next time she feels anxious about her singleness, she is going to meditate on a strategic Bible verse. Philippians 4:13 will remind her she already has access to the only relationship that can truly bring contentment, joy, and peace: her relationship with Jesus. After rereading that verse, she will pray, asking God for his strength and to help her trust his timing.

So, here's Ashley's whole TRUTH:

T   Trigger: Seeing someone's engagement pictures on Instagram.

R   Root Beliefs and Values: A life of singleness is not a life worth living.

U   Unpleasant Emotion: Anxiety about singleness.

T   Truth from God's Word: A relationship with Christ is what makes life worth living.

H   Helpful Future Response: Meditate on Philippians 4:13 and ask God for strength and patience.

Checking Under the Hood

A counselor I was seeing encouraged me to do this exercise to help work through some of my own anxiety. Around the time I was seeing him, our world was still in the early stages of the COVID-19 pandemic response. I mentioned that the local restrictions on large-group gatherings were causing me anxiety about my ministry.

My anxious thoughts were, *What if the ministry I lead doesn't come back the way it was? What if we never again have three thousand young adults meeting in person and thousands more streaming from satellite locations?*

I knew the "U" was "anxiety about not meeting" and the "T" was "local restrictions on meetings." What I didn't know was why. I had not identified the root beliefs informing my fears.

As I talked with my counselor, he asked about what would happen if my ministry didn't return to normal. I told him I would feel like I had failed. As I shared, it became clear that *my ministry's* success is how I determine *my* success. I had a root belief that my worth and identity came from my ministry.

He reminded me of the truth from God's Word that my identity as a person has nothing to do with my ministry. My ministry will come and go. My worth and identity come from being a child of God (see Galatians 4:7).

As I began to rehearse that simple truth, I felt peace wash over me. I felt less afraid of what might happen and less panicked over the fact that we were not meeting. Now when those moments pop up, I remind myself, *No matter what happens to the ministry I lead, that's not where I find my identity and worth. They come from who God says I am: his child. Nothing compares to that.* So, here's my full TRUTH journal:

T Trigger: Government restrictions on large groups, with no end in sight.

R Root Beliefs and Values: My identity is in the ministry I lead. If *it's* not a success, *I'm* not a success.

U Unpleasant Emotion: Anxiety about my ministry not returning to what it had been if large-group gatherings are not allowed in the near future.

T Truth from God's Word: My identity is not in what I do; it's in being God's son.

H Helpful Future Response: When anxious feelings about my ministry come, I will remember that whatever happens to the ministry I lead, my identity and worth don't have any connection to that; they come from God.

Only by taking the time to get to the specific beliefs that were fueling my anxiety could I allow the truth from God's Word to combat them and prepare me for future moments when those fears pop up again.

This isn't a one-and-done exercise but rather a tool meant to help expose the lies that often feed our anxious emotions and push us to the truth from God's Word. I hope the next time you feel anxious that this will help you at least take steps to work through what beliefs are behind your feelings and what God has to say about them.

Part II
Thou Shalt Not Freak Out

3

Dog Moms

Trusting God with What We Need

Dog moms, bro. You've heard of soccer moms. There is now a grow-ing phenomenon in our culture called *dog moms*. A dog mom is just what you think. They don't see themselves as a pet owner; they see themselves as a dog mother. They spoil their fur babies with love and affection as though the animals were their own children. They're known for arranging dog playdates with other dog moms, providing their dogs gourmet food, giving them presents at Christmas, dress-ing them in winter sweaters, and the list goes on. A good friend of mine is a pretty extreme example of this. I don't want to name names, but her name is Emily.

She's the most intense dog mom I've ever met. She really thinks of her dogs as children. I remember her once saying, "Every time I go to Target, it's an opportunity to buy a new toy for my little baby." She has her dog's Halloween costume picked out months in ad-vance. Yes, dog costumes. They are a thing.

Emily even gives her dogs *middle* names. If you are from the South, you have met someone with a double name. She might say, "Hey, my name is Mary Claire," but then you call her Mary and she'll quickly correct you by saying, "It's Mary Claire." Emily does the same thing with her dogs. "This is Cooper James." Don't even think about calling him just Cooper. If you do, expect Emily to get a little salty: "It's actually Cooper James." Dog middle names. It's really come to this.

The lengths to which Emily will go to provide for her dogs is astounding. Why? Because she really loves her dogs. (There may also be a bit of psychosis involved, but you didn't hear that from me. All I said was she really loves her dogs.)

With that in mind, let me ask you a question. Ready?

Do you think she loves her dogs more than God loves you? Do you think she *thinks* about her dogs more than God thinks about you? Do you think she *values* her dogs more than God values you? My guess is you would say, "No, of course not."

But for many of us, our mentality is not *I have a loving Father who is going to care for me.* More often it resembles *If I don't do enough, everything is going to fall apart.*

Bird Watching

In the middle of Jesus's sermon about anxiety, he addressed a similar issue with his audience:

> Look at the birds of the air; they do not sow or reap or store away in barns, and yet your heavenly Father feeds them. *Are you not much more valuable than they?* (Matthew 6:26)

When Jesus said this, he was teaching outside. My guess is that he looked up, saw some birds flying in the sky, and thought, *Let me show them what I mean.*

He says, "Look at those birds flying up there." At which point everyone thought, *Oh no!* and started covering their heads. Jesus continues, "Do you know what birds don't do? They don't plant crops and pluck them at harvest. They don't carefully save food for the future. Yet God provides for them." Remember, his audience saved food for the future because they were anxious about having enough.

To us he might say, "Look at those birds. They don't have to contribute to a 401(k) for their retirement. They don't keep a calendar to manage their to-dos, or a budget to get out of debt. They don't have a Hinge or Bumble profile to find a spouse. They don't do any of the responsible things you do, yet God takes care of them."

It's almost like Jesus is telling us, "The birds of the air barely even try. They fly around and look for a worm or seed to eat. At some point, they see another bird and think, *She's kind of hot. I should mate with her.* Then they decide, *We should go south since it's getting cold.* One asks, 'Should we decide *where* south? Should we reserve an Airbnb?' Then they both laugh and the other one says, 'Naw. We'll figure it out when we get there.'" Birds are borderline irresponsible, yet God provides for them.

Which brings us back to Jesus's question:

> Are you not much more valuable [to God] than they?

I love this question. In Jesus's day, birds were among the *least* valuable animals around. Later, Jesus says you could buy two for a penny:

> Are not two sparrows sold for a penny? Yet not one of them will fall to the ground outside your Father's care. And even the very hairs of your head are all numbered. So don't be afraid; you are worth more than many sparrows. (10:29–31)

For just a penny, you could get two birds! Now, I am not the best at math, but based on my calculations, the value of a bird would have been . . . wait, I think I figured it out . . . *half* a penny.

Think about Jesus's question: "Are you not more valuable to God than a bird?" Or, for you econ majors, "Are you not worth more to God than half a penny?"

You are a human made in God's image. He created some incredible things, but nothing else even comes close to you—yes, *you*—because you were created in his image. Think about that! Compared to you, God yawns when he looks at the Grand Canyon. While God is thinking about you, if an angel points out the northern lights, he's like, "Ehhh." The Great Barrier Reef? Victoria Falls? *Not* made in God's image. Pales in comparison to you. *You* are what's valuable to God. It wasn't for birds that Jesus came into the world to give his life; it was for you.

So, if God cares enough about a bird to provide for its needs, won't he care for you?

Jesus is not telling us not to try. He's not a bizarre life coach saying, "Just sit on your hands and do nothing, and everything will come your way!" No, the Bible does not teach that. We should be diligent and work hard. But ultimately, Jesus is saying to us, "Don't put your confidence in your ability to provide for yourself or in your ability to predict the future; put your confidence in God."

You can rest in God's provision.

Designer Clothing

Jesus makes the same point when he brings up the idea of flowers and clothes. He says,

> Why do you worry about clothes? See how the flowers of the field grow. They do not labor or spin. Yet I tell you that not even Solomon in all his splendor was dressed like one of these. (6:28-29)

Jesus looks around and points to the flowers growing in the field. He says, "Look how beautiful those flowers are. Not even King Solomon had clothes that were as impressive." In case you could use a refresher, Solomon was the king of Israel about a thousand years before Jesus. He was rich and was known to have a taste for the finer things in life. Solomon was the dude on *MTV Cribs* showing off his posh mansion and garage full of Lambos.

Remember your senior year of high school when you voted on who in your class should win different superlatives? There was "most athletic," "most likely to succeed," and "most likely to be famous." (I did not win "most likely to ruin his lawn," but I should have.) Well, if the Bible did one of those, the winner for "best dressed" would have been, without question, King Solomon.

Still, as fresh as his wardrobe was, it paled in comparison to the artistry and elegance of the flowers in the field.

Jesus continues,

> If that is how God clothes the grass of the field, which is here today and tomorrow is thrown into the fire, will he not much more clothe you? (verse 30)

We all have been there. You brought flowers home, admired their beauty, and then threw them in the fire. (I'm kidding. I think only sociopaths do that. Hopefully, you've never done that.)

So, why did Jesus say people would burn flowers? The word *fire* is translated from a Greek word that means "oven."[1] Back then, when you wanted to bake something, you built a fire inside an oven. The kindling for that fire was usually made of dried grass and flowers gathered from nearby fields. In other words, a husband coming home with roses was bringing home cooking supplies. He'd say, "Look, honey, I brought you kindling!"

This anecdote shows how Jesus's flower illustration proves his point. If God will dress up the ground with beautiful flowers that live for a day and then are destroyed, won't he clothe and care for his very own children?

Your heavenly Father *will* provide for your needs.

Jesus Jokes (Little Faither)

In my opinion, the greatest comedic TV show of all time is *Seinfeld*. Every time I watch an episode, I find myself laughing at the hilarious and relatable exchanges between Jerry, George, Kramer, and Elaine. (If you like the show, my guess is we'd be friends. If you don't, I'm praying for you . . . and all the Android users out there.)

In an episode titled "The Raincoats,"[2] a new guy is dating Elaine. His greatest flaw is immediately obvious. He is a *close talker*. What is a close talker? Someone who gets uncomfortably right in your face when talking to you. Forget about personal space. You can feel their hot breath as they're speaking. Elaine eventually considers this a deal breaker and ends the relationship. (Other reasons for breakups in the show include eating peas individually, not using exclamation points, and a woman having "man hands." Now if you need a reason to break up with your boo, you've got a few new options. That might be worth the price of this book!)

The term *close talker* is hilarious for a couple of reasons. Most of us have someone who is a close talker, who has no sense of how awkwardly close they are to you when they talk. Whoever that person is for you, I just pray they don't eat a lot of garlic. If you don't know who that person is in your life, *you* may be that person. (Just saying.)

Also, it's an invented expression but takes no explaining. *Close talker* is not a term you will find in the dictionary, but you don't need to. It explains itself.

In Matthew 6, right in the middle of explaining about God's provision, Jesus invents his own phrase, one that similarly has some comedic genius to it and requires no explanation: "You of little faith" (verse 30).

The word meaning "you of little faith" (ὀλιγόπιστοι) occurs nowhere else in Greek literature before this and is used only by Jesus in the Bible. Scholars believe Jesus just made up the word.[3] He took the two Greek words for "little" and "to have faith," threw them together, and made *little faither*. Just as the show *Seinfeld* did with *close talker*.

It's almost as if Jesus is being comedic, trying to help them see how crazy it is to believe what they claim about God *and*, simultaneously, be anxious. It's like he is saying, *You believe God created everything—the birds, all of creation, the heavens, moon, stars, and yet he doesn't have what it takes to provide for you? You're a bunch of "little faithers."*

In a lighthearted way, Jesus introduces a powerful truth. There is a direct relationship between the size of your *faith* and the size of your *worry*.

Just like those Jesus was speaking to, *we* believe great things about God but struggle to think he cares for our basic needs. Thankfully, Jesus isn't done yet. Next, he gives his audience the reason not to be anxious.

Who's Your Daddy?

Imagine if I'm hanging out with you and say, "Hey, let's go to lunch. Come on. It will be great. You can ride with me. I'll drive." As we're heading there, you say, "Oh man. I forgot my wallet!"

I respond with, "Don't worry about it."

We get to lunch. We're eating our food, hanging out. When we're done, the waiter asks, "One check or two?"

I reply, "Two checks."

You would look at me and ask, "What do you mean, two checks? You said not to worry about it. I told you I didn't have my wallet!"

If I respond with, "Oh, you thought I was going to pay for you? No. I just didn't want you to worry. Worry is never fun. I was just trying to encourage you," you would probably say, "You're a bad friend and a little crazy." You would be right.

Let me ask you a question I hope might flip the script on your anxiety. Could God be a good God and say, "Do not worry, but I *don't* have you covered"? Of course not! Over and over, Jesus tells us, "Do not worry." What's his reasoning? How can we possibly not worry?

We have a heavenly Father who will provide for us. He says,

> Do not worry, saying, "What shall we eat?" or "What shall we drink?" or "What shall we wear?" For the pagans run after all these things, and your heavenly Father knows that you need them. (verses 31-32)

The word *pagan* is another way of describing people who are not Christians or who don't have a relationship with God. Jesus is saying, "Remember, you are different from the pagans. You have a heavenly Father who promises to meet all your needs. Remember who your Father in heaven is. He knows what you need and has promised to provide."

How far would God go to provide for you? He sent his only Son to die in your place on a cross. There is no length our God will not go in order to provide for his children.

As Christians, the irony of worrying through this life is that we have trusted God with our eternal lives. So to be anxious is like saying, "God, I trust you with all my eternity, just not with my presentation on Thursday."

Work hard. Be responsible. Prepare for the presentation. Fill out the application. Get your clever Jedi-mind-trick answers ready for when the interviewer asks you about your weaknesses.

Do all the right things you should do. But at the end of the day, remember who your heavenly Father is. He is the One who has promised, "I've got you. I will meet your needs. You can ride with me. I'll pay." Just like everyone else, Christians don't know what the future holds. But we know the One who holds the future. Remember who your Father is and what he has promised.

The Second-Most-Repeated Command in the Bible

If we gave Olympic medals for the most repeated commands in the Bible, "Fear not" would take the gold. What command would take home the silver?

"Remember."

God wants his people to remember. Remember who their God is. Remember his promises. Remember what he has done. Remember what he can do and will do. He commands us to remember. He probably says it so often because we are people with short attention spans who forget what we had for breakfast, let alone who God is.

Jesus tells his audience, "Remember who you are—you are children of God—and who your heavenly Father is. He loves you and will provide for you."

Remember Emily the dog mom? To be honest, it's not hard for me to believe that God loves me more than Emily loves her dogs.

But you know what is hard for me to believe? That according to the Bible there is no parent who loves their children more than God loves you (see 7:11). Of all the truths in the Bible, this is one of the hardest for me to believe. Why? I have a four-year-old son named Crew and a two-year-old daughter named Monroe. (We call her Mo-Mo. She is a firecracker!)

To say I love them is an understatement. I would do anything to provide for them, care for them, and protect them. Because they are kids? No. Because they are *my* kids.

How much I love them can almost make me irrationally protective. Recently, my wife and son came home after his swim lessons. They walked into the house and I asked, "How did it go?"

She responded, "He didn't like it. He didn't have a great attitude, and he wasn't really able to do the drills like the other kids."

I immediately snapped into a protective mode that didn't even make sense, as if I were now personally insulted by swim lessons. I was thinking, *Really? Oh really?! Swim lessons are bothering my son. Who exactly do "swim lessons" think they are? Why do people even need to swim? Swimming is stupid! We don't live by the ocean. He doesn't need to swim.*

Eventually, I realized the absurdity of mentally picking a fight with swim lessons as though they were some bully at school. But it's hard not to, because I love my son.

Your heavenly Father loves you far more than any parent has ever loved their child. Next time you find yourself anxious, remember God's love and his promise to provide for your needs. Does that mean you will get everything you want every time? No. But he will provide for your needs.

Yeah, David, but what if I'm worried about things beyond just my needs?

Good question, because many of our worries are not about things we *need* but rather things we *want*. That's exactly what Jesus covers next.

4

One Percent Chance

Surrendering the Unknown

With a single sentence, our world changed. "Your daughter has been flagged for a chromosomal disorder that, if present, would mean she has only a one percent chance of surviving."

Three months earlier, my wife and I found out we were pregnant. Or, more accurately, *she* was pregnant, but I am taking a little credit.

We weren't a little excited about adding to our family; we were *stoked*. We immediately announced the news to our family and friends, began to plan out which room would be the nursery, estimated how our baby's summer arrival would change our existing vacation plans, and started to pick out potential names—which is always a nearly impossible process. So many names quickly moved to the "not an option" list. We had to eliminate names of people each of us dated, names that rhyme with body parts, names of people we didn't like in high school, names that sound like curse words, and names recently used by someone we knew. The list got short incredibly fast!

Pregnant women have to go to the doctor a lot. On one of my wife's routine visits, the doctor gave her a blood test to check the health of the baby, and that would also allow us to know the gender. Standard-procedure stuff.

Then, two weeks later at nine thirty on a Wednesday night in early December, my wife's cell phone rang. She called me into our bedroom. I could tell something was wrong. She gestured to the phone and said, "It's my doctor. It's about the baby." I sat down next to her. She put the phone on speaker so I could hear.

Let me hit pause really quick. I don't know much about the medical field (my knowledge is limited to what I read on the WebMD app), but I know having a doctor call at nine thirty at night is not normal. The doctor wasn't just calling to catch up and ask, "What are your plans for the holidays?"

The doctor said, "We got the blood-test results back and found out you're having a girl. The reason we know is because she's been flagged for a chromosomal disorder unique to girls. If she has it, there's a 99 percent chance she's going to die before making it out of the womb. If she's in the one percent who make it out of the womb, she's going to need immediate heart surgery or a heart transplant. She will have severe complications for the rest of her life. She will have physical abnormalities, never be able to have kids, and not live a normal life."

You know when you watch a bomb go off in a movie and all you hear is loud ringing and then deafening silence? That's what it felt like. I was in shock. Fear, sadness, confusion, and anxiety flooded my heart. That night began a desperate journey. For the next six months, we prayed every day, "God, we don't want our baby girl to die. Will you please allow our baby girl to live?" There was nothing I wanted more than for our baby to live.

Honestly, most of our worries are about our wants, not our needs: I *want* to be married by a certain age. I *want* to get the job. I *want* to be able to pay off my student loans. I *want* to be healthy. I *want* to be able to have kids. I *want* to be successful. I *want* people to accept me. Whether I *need* those things is irrelevant; they are what I *want*. Our wants are our hopes, dreams, and desires. The thought of them not happening understandably creates anxiety.

At some point in your life, you will be confronted with things not going how you want them to. For us, we desperately *wanted* our daughter to be okay. Was it possible not to *be* overwhelmed with fear and panic at the thought she might not be? Turns out it was.

The Most Misunderstood Verse on Anxiety

After explaining that God will provide for our needs (see Matthew 6:31–32), Jesus gives an answer to the question "But what about my *wants*, Jesus?" He lays out a *remedy* so helpful and practical that it has been absolutely transformative in my life:

> Seek first the kingdom of God and his righteous-
> ness, and all these things will be added to you.
> (verse 33, ESV)

The idea of "Seek first" is pretty straightforward. It means to place something as your highest value or embrace it as the first priority in your life. That's clear.

But we're to do that with "the kingdom of God"? What exactly does that mean? Like, how do I seek heaven? And how does that help with my anxiety?

I think many of us have misunderstood this verse. Maybe you thought Jesus was saying, "Don't worry; just go on a mission trip," or, "Don't worry; just read your Bible more," or, "Don't worry; just go to church." All of which are great things to do, but if that's your takeaway, you miss the power of what Jesus says in this verse.

The word *kingdom* throughout the New Testament is the Greek word *basileia*. That word does not refer to a geographical place on the map but to the dominion or reign of a king.[1] In this case, that King is God.

So, what Jesus is really telling us is to *place God's will, God's agenda, and God's desires as the first priority for our lives* and that if we do, we will begin to experience peace. Why?

Because at the core of almost all our anxiety is a fear of things not going the way *we want*. What's another word for having things go the way I want? It's my *will* for my life. Or we could say it's my *agenda*. Want another word? How about this: It's my *kingdom*.

When I worry, it's almost always about David's kingdom, David's agenda, David's desires, David's wants. *Where will I live? How will I afford to pay the bills? How can I ensure my health and my family's health?*

This may surprise you, but I have never once lost sleep over when any of my friends will get married. I have thought about it. I have prayed for them. I care. But I have never felt anxious. Why? Because it's hard to manufacture the emotion of anxiety. It hits us or it doesn't, and it almost always hits us when it's something related to *our* kingdom.

Again, to be clear, by *our kingdom* I mean the plans, desires, and agendas we have for our own lives.

Since we're being honest, I have also never found myself anxious about whether God has what it takes to fulfill *his* plans and agendas in our world. *God, I'm just worried about all the people in Asia who are not Christians. I don't know if you've got what it takes to save them. I'm just concerned.*

It's never happened. I certainly care about them, but I have never experienced anxious feelings related to them.

I worry about *my* kids, *my* finances, *my* future. What does all that have in common? *Me!* My anxious feelings are *not* about God's agenda for my life but mine. But Jesus says, "If you will *release* your will and agenda and embrace God's as the first priority in your life, even when it contradicts yours, you will begin to experience peace."

That sounds good, really good. But for it to happen, we must understand how.

Carriage Rides

I recently went on a horse-carriage tour of the historic area in Charleston, South Carolina. We were on a family vacation and had been told that going on one of these tours was a must. So, we all ended up sitting in a carriage behind a couple of large horses and a man dressed like he lived in colonial days. I don't know who I felt worse for: the horses pulling the carriage or the guy dressed in a white colonial wig in ninety-plus-degree weather.

Like a flight attendant, the man first went through some instructions we all were to follow while on the tour. "Please keep your hands and arms inside the carriage. Please remain seated throughout the ride. No eating or drinking on the ride. When exiting the carriage, to avoid being kicked, do not walk close to the horse's back legs. Do not attempt to feed the horses."

There probably were a few more instructions, but it's really hard to take seriously a guy wearing what looked like a Benjamin Franklin costume from Party City.

It turns out each tour does not follow the same route. The tour guide is not assigned the route until everyone is on board. Why? There are so many tours taking place at the same time that they have to make sure to avoid . . . horse traffic. (I'm not sure if that's the technical term for it, as I come from a world without . . . horse traffic.)

Each carriage ride is synced into a schedule the carriage company tells only the tour guide. This means you can't predict or select what tour you are going to be placed on. You can't even pick what area of town you'd like to see. You just wait and see where your driver takes you.

Let me ask you this: What is a tour guide's agenda for everyone who goes on his carriage ride? Is it the instructions he gives, or is it the route he plans to take his passengers on?

It's *both*. He wants everyone to follow his earlier instructions while he takes them on a tour with turns and stops that only he knows.

God's agenda in our lives works the same way. Yes, it includes instructions he wants us to follow to protect us and help us along on the journey. Thankfully, we get those instructions from the Bible, not from a man wearing tights and wooden shoes (because, how weird would that be?).

God's agenda for our lives also includes a route he is guiding us through, with various stops along the way. We don't know the turns the route will take, but *God* knows, and he is the most trustworthy tour guide out there.

If we can learn to release our plans and embrace God's, even when they contradict ours, we will begin to experience peace.

Release and Embrace

The art of releasing your agenda doesn't mean pretending you don't have one. God loves you and wants you to express your hopes and desires to him.

Seeking God's kingdom first means choosing to trust him and want what he wants, whether or not it includes everything we want. After all, God is sovereign, which means he is in control of everything. If he doesn't want me to get the job, I am *not* getting the job. If he doesn't want me to be married, I am *not* going to be married. If he wants my wife to have a baby while I am out of the country, it *is* going to happen. I am not going to prevent God's plans.

Maybe you need a job. You have done everything you can to find one, but no luck. You finally find one that would be a good fit. You apply and interview. Then you find yourself waiting to hear if you got the job. Embracing God's agenda looks like going to him in prayer and saying something like, "God, you know how desperately I need this job. If I don't get it, I don't know what I am going to do. Please let me get it. But if I don't because it's not your will, I trust you. Amen."

Perhaps you are single and feel like all your friends are getting married, so you are anxious about whether or not you ever will. For you, releasing and embracing looks like praying, "God, I feel like my options for marriage are getting fewer and fewer by the day. I want a godly spouse. Will you please let marriage be part of my story? But if that is not the case, I trust you. I don't want to be single forever, but if that's what you have planned for me, I trust you."

Release your plans, embrace God's, and in return, you will get peace.

Learning to release what we want and embrace what God wants is essential because eventually life *won't* go the way we want. Maybe you don't get into the graduate school you wanted. The cancer comes back. The relationship doesn't work out. Your parents get divorced. You get laid off.

Life deals us cards we didn't ask for. In those moments, we have two options: we choose to trust God's plan and receive peace, or not trust him and receive worry. Saying it another way:

> Not have everything we want and . . . worry.
> Not have everything we want and . . . have peace.

Having everything we want in life is *not* an option, but thankfully, peace is.

When Jesus Was Overwhelmed

Jesus didn't just teach others to release their agendas and embrace God's; he did it himself. He put this principle into practice on the most anxiety-producing night of his life.

Have you ever thought about your future and felt overwhelmed? Jesus knows how that feels. I can't imagine what he felt in those hours before he was to be arrested, tortured, and crucified, being separated for the first time from his heavenly Father in the process. Jesus saw all that coming and said, "My soul is overwhelmed" (Mark 14:34). What do you do in a moment like that?

Jesus prayed. What he prayed is the ultimate example of releasing one's wants and choosing to want what God wants:

> He fell to the ground and prayed that if possible the hour might pass from him. "*Abba,* Father," he said, "everything is possible for you. Take this cup from me. *Yet not what I will, but what you will.*" (verses 35-36)

Jesus says, "God, you can do anything. Please allow another way. I don't want to die on the cross and be separated from you. But if that's your will, I trust you. I trust your agenda, even when it contradicts my own."

When you find yourself overwhelmed with anxiety, pray. Turn to

God and express your desires to him, but embrace a posture that says, *Your will before mine, God.* That posture produces peace.

So, what are you anxious about? What are you afraid may or may not happen? Are you willing to trust God with whatever he has in store? Trusting him with whatever it is won't change what he is going to do, but it will change *you.*

Two Options

As I began this chapter, I told you about the nightmare of hearing that our daughter had been flagged for a disorder that meant she had a 99 percent chance of never living outside the womb. We found that out when my wife was three months pregnant. We were told there was no way of confirming whether our baby actually had the disorder until she was born—*if* she made it that far.

We spent the next six desperate months praying for God to spare our daughter. "God, we want our daughter to live. Please let her be okay. But whatever you have for us and for her, we trust you."

I felt so out of control. I could not decide if she was going to live, I could not decide when she would be born, and I could not decide what things would look like if she survived.

What I could decide is if I would trust God.

Would I keep my white-knuckle grip on my agenda even though in actuality I could not control anything? Or would I release my plans and embrace God's plan, whatever it might be? Two options:

> I could not be in control and have worry.
> I could not be in control and have peace.

Either way, I am *not* in control. But if I release what I want and embrace what God wants, I can have peace instead of panic.

I wish I could tell you that every moment during those six months was marked by peace. I can't. I have to admit that I'm not sure I can even say that *most* of those moments were marked by peace. But I *can* say that every moment we experienced peace was a moment when I expressed our desire for our daughter to be healthy but that we would trust God's will. We prayed a thousand versions of, "God, we want our baby girl to be okay. But whatever your will for her is, we trust you. Your will and kingdom comes before ours."

I want to say that again: every moment of peace I had, struggling through the worst time of our lives, came when I practiced Jesus's invitation to pour out my desires to God and trust his will, even when it could contradict mine.

When you're confronted with fears about life not going the way you want, what will you choose? To release your kingdom so you can seek his, or to stay in charge of your kingdom even though you're not really controlling anything? Will you choose the path that leads to peace, or the one that leads to the avenue of anxiety?

Six months after that phone call, our daughter, Monroe Eloise Marvin, was born healthy and without any disorder. Either it had been a false positive or God had delivered us a miracle. I don't share that to suggest that if you just pray enough, the disorder will go away. That's not always true. God doesn't promise that things will always go the way we want them to; he promises us his peace, both now and for eternity.

5

Gift Registries

Trading Our Panic for Peace

Jesus taught that it is better to give than to receive, which is totally true (see Acts 20:35). But it's also pretty nice to receive. If you have not yet had a wedding or a baby, you need to know that the best part is the gift registry. Free gifts!

Okay, maybe it's not the best part. No, it's not the best part. I repent of the third sentence in this chapter. The best part is the spouse and the baby.

But a very close second is that you get to tell people to give you free gifts and even choose what gifts they give. A gift registry is the list you put together from certain stores of the gifts you want people to give you. Why would they give you gifts? Because you put in the hard work of getting married or having a baby! That ain't easy, but somebody's gotta do it. And you did it, so you register for the gifts you want as your reward. You then let your friends and family know where they should go to buy you your presents.

It may be the world's most passive-aggressive way of gift receiving. You are essentially telling people, "Look, don't worry about getting us anything, unless you love us. Also, if you do get us a gift, we've already chosen what it will be." Gift registries are amazing, especially if you are on the receiving end. It may be the only time in life you can make *specific requests* of what people will give you and not come off like an entitled brat.

As if that weren't great enough, technology makes registering for gifts maybe the most enjoyable shopping experience ever. You go into the store and they hand you a laser gun to scan the bar codes of any item you want to add to your registry. You walk around the store shooting at kitchenware like you are blasting opponents in a game of laser tag. I think they added the gun to make spending an afternoon at Bed Bath & Beyond more exciting for the grooms registering with their future wives. It's brilliant; they made picking out gifts feel like a game of *Call of Duty* on Xbox.

You may not have made a gift registry yet, but you *have* been asked to make requests of what you want. Throughout the Bible, God invites us to bring our requests to him. Just like with a gift registry, we are not guaranteed to get everything we ask for, but we are called to let God know our requests in prayer.

God wants to hear from you!

Let Your Requests Be Known

In the fourth chapter of his letter to the Philippians, the apostle Paul wrote,

> Do not be anxious about anything, but in everything by prayer and supplication with thanksgiving *let your requests be made known* to God. And the peace of God, which surpasses all understanding, will guard your hearts and your minds in Christ Jesus. (verses 6–7, ESV)

When I read verses like these, they almost seem too good to be true. I think, *Paul, are you saying if I just pray about things, I won't have anxiety anymore? Because I have tried praying and I am still freaking out!*

How could Paul claim such a thing? Is it possible he knew something we don't or had some special way of praying? Or maybe he said this because he didn't really have anything to be anxious about?

Before we dive deeper into Paul's words, let's understand his circumstances. Sometimes we read Bible verses like "Do not be anxious about anything" and assume whoever wrote them has no idea how stressful living in modern times is.

He's never faced the challenge of online dating, car payments, student loans, retirement savings, or comparison on social media. He's never struggled to find affordable housing, handled jerk bosses making unrealistic demands, received the news that his parents are getting divorced, or lived through a worldwide quarantine. *So, sure, Paul, it's easy for you to write about how prayer is the antidote to anxiety, because you have no idea what stress is really like.*

Not true. I mean, like . . . Really. Not. True.

If anyone had reason to be anxious, it was Paul.

Paul wrote the book of Philippians in AD 62 from a tiny, cold, dark Roman jail cell he was thrown into for the crime of talking about Jesus. A historian of the time described Paul's cell as a place of "neglect, darkness, and stench" with "a hideous and terrifying appearance."[1]

At the time of his writing, Paul is probably in his late fifties. He is cold and hungry, and his eyesight is getting weaker by the day.[2] He is waiting to hear his fate and anticipating it could be the punishment of death.[3] *That's* Paul's situation when he writes to the Christians in the city of Philippi.

As he leans against the dungeon wall, he feels the scars covering his back from receiving the notorious thirty-nine lashes (torture that killed many people) *five* different times throughout his life,[4] not to mention the toll taken on his body from having been shipwrecked, beaten with rods on three occasions, stoned and left for dead, and starved.[5] He faces that physical torture in addition to public ridicule and persecution, all because he is trying to spread the gospel. Paul also has the stress of whether the new churches he has started will succeed and if the people he led to Jesus will continue in the faith.

If I had the option of trading my problems for Paul's, that would be a hard pass. I'm guessing you'd rather have *your* problems than his too. Paul was in *that* jail cell, in *those* circumstances, when he wrote those verses. Here is the first part again:

> Do not be anxious about anything, but in every-
> thing by prayer and supplication with thanksgiving
> let your requests be made known to God. (verse 6,
> ESV)

Paul says that every time you feel anxious about something, talk to God about it. Tell him what you are afraid of, nervous about, worried over, or distracted by and what you desire to happen. If something is important enough to worry about, it's important enough to pray about.

I find it interesting that Paul says the same thing three times in one verse. He uses three different phrases that all essentially mean the same thing:

- He says go to God in *prayer.* (What is prayer? Talking to God.)
- And in *supplication.* (What is supplication? It means to ask God for something. Or . . . talking to God.)
- And to *let your requests be made known to God.* (What does that mean? Tell God what you want.)

What Paul says in verse 6 is that when you are anxious, you should talk to God about it, talk to God about it, and talk to God about it. So, why is this so often *not* what we do in the face of anxiety? I think it's because we don't know God the way Paul did.

Pretend Prayer

Is it possible you think of God as some distant figure you can talk to but only about biblical things? Maybe you assume you shouldn't bother God with everyday worries and fears. So, you wouldn't go to him with things like, *God, I'm anxious that I won't get the internship I applied for. Please help me not be anxious and also get accepted.*

Many Christians I know think they don't have permission to be honest with God about their everyday fears, hopes, and lives. They believe prayers like these are off-limits:

- *God, I am anxious about being able to afford housing. Please allow me to make ends meet.*
- *God, I am anxious about what I will do if I don't get this job. Please let me get it.*
- *God, I am anxious about my dad's health. Please let the cancer treatment work.*
- *God, I am anxious about my autoimmune disease. Please help me trust you, and please heal me.*
- *God, I am anxious about my brother in rehab. Please help him conquer his addiction.*

We think we can't be real with God. Sometimes the way people pray even shows this. Out of nowhere, someone asked to pray will downshift into King James Version (an old, formal-sounding version of the Bible): "Our Father-eth who art in heaven-eth, today-eth make-eth it great-eth for you-eth." Praying like that is *not* genuine and it's *not* more spiritual. Honestly, it's kind of weird-eth.

Paul says you and I can talk to God about everything. You've been invited to ask, to ask, and to ask. And it's not just Paul. Another of Jesus's disciples, named Peter, says the same thing:

> Cast all your anxiety on [God] because he cares for you. (1 Peter 5:7)

Peter says to bring to God everything you care about because *you* are what he cares about. If something is important enough to worry about, it is important enough to pray about. If you are worried about it, tell God. Tell him how you feel. Tell him what you are afraid of. If your biggest takeaway from this book is "Pray honest prayers," I would consider that a win.

I've sat with people who told me, "I feel constant anxiety about still being single, but I don't want to pray, 'God, will you please bring me a spouse?' because then he won't bring me a spouse. He'll want me to learn to be content without having a spouse before he gives me one."

Why do we think that maneuvering works on God? He sees everything. He knows everything about what we want, what we don't want, and what we're trying to act like we want and don't want. We've been invited to go to him with whatever is on our minds. He cares about what we care about.

Monsters in My Room

Every now and then, in the middle of the night, my four-year-old son will come into our bedroom and wake me up with a "There's a monster underneath my bed" or "There's something scary in my closet." I tell him, "I know. I put it there to keep you from getting out of bed and waking me up at 3:00 a.m."

I'm kidding. I get up and carry him back to his bed. Then I go under his bed or in his closet to show him there is nothing there. I reassure him, "You don't have to be afraid. There are no monsters. The only thing you should be afraid of is Mommy if you don't go back to sleep."

I have to admit that part of me loves when he comes into our room. It's not because I enjoy being woken up in the middle of the night by the silhouette of a three-foot child appearing in our room like we are in a scene from the movie *The Shining*.

I love it because when my son is afraid, he's not scared to come to me. This shows me he knows I care about him not being tormented by monsters under his bed, and he believes his daddy is big enough to handle any monsters in his room.

I would be heartbroken if he didn't feel that way.

What if he thought he heard a monster in the closet or saw a shadow from under his bed and thought, *I can't bring this to my daddy. He doesn't care about me, and he certainly isn't strong enough to handle a monster. I will just stay here, alone and afraid*?

Even just the thought of that breaks my heart.

But that's exactly what we do with God. Rather than bring him our fears and concerns, knowing he cares for us and is strong enough to do something about them, we carry them around ourselves, going through life feeling alone and afraid.

That's why Paul says that when you are feeling anxious, tell your heavenly Father. He cares about you, so he cares about what you care about, and he is big enough to do something about it.

Let Them Rise

My daughter, Monroe, loves balloons. She wants every balloon, regardless of the color, but pink is her favorite. We have attended parties where she sees a balloon floating in the air and flips out about wanting it as her own. As a good parent, I, of course, help her to understand that the balloon is not for her and the importance of delayed gratification. No, that doesn't work on kids. I get her the balloon. I'm not proud of it, but I've taken decorations from birthday parties just to restore the peace. Oh, and also because I love her.

Recently, we were at a party in someone's backyard and it happened. She saw a balloon. She wanted the balloon. The problem was that this balloon was filled with helium. I'm not sure how much you know about two-year-olds, but following instructions like "Hold this string or the balloon will fly into the sky" is not really their thing.

So, thirty seconds after I handed Monroe the balloon, it was sailing into the sky, headed for wherever balloons go. As you might guess, she wanted another one. Realizing this would keep happening until there were no balloons left at this party, I took the string holding the new balloon and tied it around my daughter's wrist. Even if she let it go, it wouldn't go far.

The expression "*Let* your requests be made known to God" is more passive than an active command such as "*Make* your requests known." It holds the idea that your worries want to rise up to God like a balloon filled with helium and you just need to let them, because you were not meant to carry them.

Chances are that at some point today, you were bombarded with a flood of stress, loneliness, worry, and disappointment. It may have been related to your finances, a conflict you had with a friend, a big project at work, or doubts about someone you are dating. Or maybe you have stress that there is *not* someone you are dating and therefore think there probably never will be. Those, and a thousand other anxious feelings, can pour into our hearts before we've even been awake long enough to brush our teeth.

What I love about the verses in Philippians 4 is that they're telling you it's not heroic to pretend that you're not worried. You're supposed to let your anxieties rise, not suppress them. When you experience anxious feelings, *let* them go up and rise to God through prayer.

You might be thinking, *David, I've tried praying and I feel nothing. Actually, it makes me more anxious, because I have to think about what's worrying me. Sometimes I'm so anxious I can't even pray. It's easier to get on my phone and distract myself instead. Then I don't have to think too much.*

If that describes you at all, know that I get it. I realize it's easier to avoid feelings. (I'm an Enneagram 7—avoiding feelings is what I do best.) Sure, distracting yourself may give you a feeling of relief for a moment. But if you continue to stuff your feelings and avoid your anxieties, you may spiral into a seemingly endless cycle of avoidance, anxiety, more avoidance, and more anxiety, until the anxiety becomes impossible to carry. That's because you weren't meant to carry it at all.

Avoiding anxiety will only make you more anxious, so you must acknowledge your fears and feelings. Don't run from them, but instead run to God with them. Don't be afraid. Don't panic. Pray, and remind yourself of who God is. He is good. He is in control. He sees you and cares about you. Remember what we talked about in chapters 3 and 4?

Remember who God is. Now *request* what you need.

Trading Panic for Peace

Paul says that when you are anxious, bring your requests to God and in return you will receive "the peace of God." You can trade panic for peace. That's not a bad trade. And not just any peace, but the peace of God, which surpasses our ability to understand and will guard our hearts and minds.

The phrase *will guard* was a military term used for soldiers on guard duty.[6] The Romans stationed troops in Philippi to protect their interests there. The people who received Paul's letter would understand that just as the soldiers guard their city, God's peace guards the hearts of those who bring their anxieties to him.

How does that happen? If God gave us anything and everything we asked for, sure, that would produce peace. But God doesn't, so how does bringing our anxieties to him give us peace?

I believe Paul would say that it's because, as Christians, the heart of our faith is the understanding that our heavenly Father loves us and is in control. God has control over *everything*. If we ask him for something and our request isn't answered the way we want, it's not because God is not capable or doesn't care; it's because he knows something we don't.

Off the Registry

Remember those wedding and baby registries? Here is something tragic you should know. Despite your best passive-aggressive attempts to let people know what gifts you want, inevitably someone will decide to buy something *off the registry*. Someone who sees your list will think, *Yeah, I'm not getting any of these. I've got something else in mind.*

Often when someone goes off the registry, you end up with something you didn't ask for and might never use. We're talking matching homemade sweaters, decorative pictures you put in the attic, silverware that doesn't match the set you have, and the list goes on. While the person means well, there's a good chance he or she is just not very good at giving gifts you truly want or need. (Sorry,

Aunt Betty.) (Side note: I don't literally have an Aunt Betty, but don't we all have a figurative one?)

Sometimes I think we feel the same way about the circumstances of our lives. We get handed things we never asked for—we don't get accepted into the school we wanted, we lose our job, the relationship doesn't work out, or a family member gets sick. Is it because God doesn't care? Or, like that one aunt we all have, is he just not great at giving gifts?

Aunt Betty is not the only one who gives you gifts that aren't on the registry. There is another type of person who goes off the registry—not because the individual is bad at giving gifts, but because he or she is a little further down the road than you are. The person has been married or has had kids for a while, and that person looks at your list and thinks, *They don't know to ask for this, but they're going to need it.*

This happened when we had our baby shower for our first child a few years ago. We sent our list out to everyone, but at the party, some friends told us they bought us something that wasn't on our registry. It was a particular type of bassinet (which is basically a small crib). They said, "You don't even know to ask for this, but when the baby is screaming at three in the morning, this is the bassinet you're going to want. Just trust us."

Essentially, they were saying, "You don't even know to ask for it, but because we've been there, because we've seen it, because we know what's coming, we know this is what you're going to need."

We smiled, but we were thinking, *Why didn't you just give us the things we asked for?*

Two months into unsuccessfully trying to get our son to sleep, we remembered the bassinet. The one we didn't ask for and were a little insulted by. That one.

Sleep deprivation will open you up to trying anything. We put him in there and . . . he slept like a champ. It was a game changer! We never would have asked for that present, but our friends knew what we didn't know. They knew better.

God works in our lives in a similar way. When he doesn't answer our prayers the way we hoped or puts something in our lives we didn't want, it's as if he's saying, *You don't even know what you need, but I love you and will bring the right things into your life—things you don't even know to ask for but would if you knew what I know.*

Pastor Timothy Keller put it this way: "God will either give us what we ask or give us what we would have asked if we knew everything he knew."[7]

Why? Because he's a good Father. He loves you and he gives only good things. He proved his love when he gave you the best thing by sending his Son to die in your place.

When he doesn't give you what you request, he knows something that you don't. You can trust him. So, when worries come up, let them rise up. Bring your requests to God, and rest in the peace only he can give you.

6

Subway to Somewhere

Changing How We Think

A few years ago, my wife, Calli, and I went to New York City for the weekend to celebrate our wedding anniversary. We went in December, when the city is alive with decorations for Christmas and packed with tourists. (Pro tip: You *have* to go see the Rockefeller Center Christmas tree, but only if you can tolerate ridiculous crowds.)

There's lots to love about New York, but one of the things I especially appreciate is the transportation system—specifically, the subway, for a couple of reasons. First, using it makes you feel like a native New Yorker, not some poser from Texas. Second, it's unbelievably cheap. For just a few bucks, you can go anywhere in the city you want. Compared to Uber, they are practically giving free rides away.

During our trip, we planned to meet some friends for dinner in another part of town. Since we love the subway (and didn't want to pay ten times the price for a taxi), we headed to the closest subway station. We had to figure out which train to take and quickly discovered that iPhone maps don't exactly work great underground, so instead we pulled out the old-fashioned paper subway map our hotel gave us.

After spending way too much time trying to figure out what all the different-colored lines on the map meant, we realized the subway train we needed wasn't working. We'd have to take a different route to our destination. We were confused. *Do we take the F train? Do we take the A train? What do we do?* We had to get it right because the train we took would determine our direction and destination.

By this point in the book, you have probably realized that I am a guy, and well, we guys don't normally love asking for directions. It might make us seem weak. So I didn't ask. With confidence, my wife and I hopped on a train, thinking we were heading to downtown Manhattan.

We were actually going toward Brooklyn. We were headed entirely in the wrong direction and didn't notice until we got farther and farther away from where we wanted to be.

What do you do in this kind of situation? If you're smart, you recognize you have to get off the wrong train. Then you get out your old-timey map again and figure out which train will take you in the *right* direction.

What does this have to do with anxiety? Not much, except *everything*. Our minds work in a similar way to a train. We even have a term for this. We call it a "train of thought." Just as a train takes you in a specific direction, our thoughts take us to a destination. Unfortunately, our thought life can take us in directions and to destinations we don't want.

Trains of Thought

Have you noticed that the thoughts you have are usually not just "one and done"? When we allow anxious thoughts to stay in our minds, they invite other thoughts like them to join. Maybe these are some "trains of thought" you have taken:

> **The WebMD Train.** All of a sudden, you have a sore back and wonder, *What could this be?* So you go on WebMD, type in your symptoms, and get results like appendix rupture, kidney failure, and cancer. (Why does it seem like cancer is always on the list of potential causes?) Before you know it, a

little back pain has you googling, "Doctors for a spinal cancer screening."

The Reading-into-the-Relationship Train. You recently started dating a guy. He drops you off after your third date. He says, "I had a nice time," and then gives you a side hug. As you walk through your front door, you start overanalyzing. *What does "nice time" mean? And a side hug? Really? What am I—his cousin?* You begin wondering if this guy even likes you. You think, *I bet there is someone else. I bet he likes Sarah.* Next thing you know, you're stalking Sarah on Instagram to see how often he is liking her pictures. Then you think, *He's probably going to break this off. You know what? I'm going to break up with him before he breaks up with me!* A couple of anxious thoughts put you on the "Break Up with Him Before He Breaks Up with Me" express. Why? Because our thoughts take us places.

The "My Boss Doesn't Like Me" Train. You send an email to your boss and don't get a response. You think, *Huh. No response. I wonder if he got the email. Wait, of course he got my email. You can't not get an email. I guess he must not have liked my idea. He probably doesn't like me!* It doesn't take long until you've decided, *I bet I'm next on the chopping block. I need to update my LinkedIn profile. Only problem is that I can never remember my password.*

The What-If Train. This may be the most common train of thought we jump on. This train looks at the future and focuses on what could potentially go wrong. *What if I get COVID-19? What if my boss fires me? What if they don't like me? What if my family dies in a plane crash? What if I never get married? What if I get a divorce? What if we break up? What if I don't get the job?* These thoughts don't just sit there; they lead to another thought, and another thought, and you go from being fine to having a total panic about your life.

One anxious thought leads to another and you find yourself spiraling down the tracks of an anxiety train ride you never wanted to take.

If we can't control our trains of thought, we are no longer in control of our lives. As we will see, the good news according to the Bible is that we can learn to control our thoughts. We can't control all the circumstances we face, but we *can* control our thoughts and how we react to them. By doing so, we can win what my friend Jennie Allen rightly calls "the greatest battle of our generation: the battle for our minds."[1]

Replace Your Trains of Thought

As I mentioned in the previous chapter, Paul wrote the book of Philippians from a prison cell. Not exactly the best of circumstances. If anyone had reason to dwell on anxious thoughts, it would be Paul. But immediately after saying not to be anxious about anything but to pray about everything (see 4:6), he writes,

> Whatever is true, whatever is honorable, whatever is just, whatever is pure, whatever is lovely, whatever is commendable, if there is any excellence, if there is anything worthy of praise, think about these things. (verse 8, ESV)

Remember, the biblical definition of being anxious is *meditating on fearful thoughts*. Paul encourages us not to meditate on *those* thoughts but to meditate on *these* thoughts. We get off the anxious trains of thought and get on positive trains of thought.

We need to meditate on (a.k.a. fill our minds with and keep thinking about) whatever is *true, noble, right, pure, lovely, admirable, excellent, and worthy of worship*, rehearsing and replaying these thoughts in our minds.

We choose to think about who God is and the truths contained in his Word. That is what we dwell on. We don't just stop thinking about the wrong things; we start thinking about the right ones.

Now, before you dismiss Paul's teaching as impractical or too good to be true, you should know he is recommending the same thing that psychologists today have people do. One of psychology's relatively recent developments is called *cognitive behavioral therapy*, or CBT. To state it simply, the goal of CBT is to address and replace *thoughts* that lead to *anxious feelings* that lead to *unhealthy behavior*. What this means is, counselors and psychologists have just recently caught up with what Paul wrote two thousand years ago!

You can replace your thoughts. If you fix your mind, you will fix your life. Or as it says in Proverbs, "As he thinks within himself, so he is" (23:7, NASB). You are what you think.

Think About Your Thoughts

Studies estimate that the average person has between 50,000 and 80,000 thoughts a day.[2] Think about that! (See what I did there? And now you've just had 80,001.)

While many of these are relatively mundane thoughts, like whether to take a shower before work or comment on your friend's social-media post, there are still many thoughts that, if you allow them, will direct you toward the path of panic and anxiety.

Think about the thoughts you've had in your mind today or over this past week.

Have your thoughts today been full of fear or full of faith? More stressed or more relaxed? Negative or positive? Thankful or discontent? Anxious or peaceful? Focused on your temporary circumstances or on God's eternal truths? Related to yourself or others?

How would you describe them?

My guess is a mixture of all of the above. But the more negative, fearful, worried, stressed, and self-centered your thoughts are, the more anxious your mind will be.

Imagine what life would look like if you really applied these verses. Consider what today could look like if you choose thoughts centered on truths from God's Word, such as:

- *God is good and in control, so I can trust him.*
- *God is for me and working everything together for good.*
- *God placed me here on purpose.*
- *I am never alone because God is with me.*
- *God will meet all my needs because he cares about me.*
- *Nothing can keep me from God's love.*
- *This life is a vapor, and my problems are small compared to what great things await me in eternity.*
- *My past doesn't define me; Christ does.*
- *I am forgiven, loved, and accepted.*

If thoughts like these were constantly on your mind, how much more peace filled would you be? How much of your negative self-talk would end? How less worried would you feel? How much better would you sleep?

What trains of thought do you need to replace? According to Paul, if you are not on the thought train of truth, purity, excellence, and worship, you are on the wrong train.

Garbage In, Garbage In

On Saturday mornings, I typically take my son with me to pick up doughnuts for the family. His go-to doughnut is whichever one is covered with icing that looks like his favorite superhero at that moment. He will also pick out a pink sprinkled doughnut for his little sister, because even though all the icing tastes the same, we have learned that if it ain't pink, she ain't eating it. I pick out some other doughnuts for my wife and me, and we head back home.

The older I get, the more I have noticed that something happens to me very shortly after eating doughnuts: I feel like garbage. Not from the shame of eating doughnuts, but because of how they make me feel: tired, bloated, and like I just ate cake for breakfast . . . because I did.

Putting garbage in your body leads to feeling like you put garbage in your body. In the same way that consuming junk food upsets your stomach, consuming junk information messes with your mind.

A crucial component of replacing your trains of thought is cutting out the sources of junk information that are fueling your anxious, fearful, and overwhelming thoughts.

Maybe your mind's junk food is social media, especially if it makes you feel anxious about how much you *don't* have compared to others or if you feel insecure about what you look like, the car you drive, the vacation you took, or the number of followers you have after scrolling. Ironically, it's common to pull up Instagram, YouTube, or TikTok to distract you from things that stress you out only to find that it feeds your anxiety.

Maybe you need to get off dating apps because you check your phone every three seconds to see if you got a match. You fill your mind with obsessive thoughts about relationships, which just fuels discontentment in your life.

Maybe your junk food is online shopping, Pinterest, or Liketoknow.it. You swipe through hundreds of pictures of designer clothes, models with perfect bodies, or women in beautiful wedding dresses. You're filling your mind with discontentment and believing that your value is in how you look or what you have. You become anxious, thinking you'll never be pretty enough or good enough.

You might fill your mind with negativity from Twitter or the news. These actually may be the worst offenders. Have you heard of doom scrolling? Yep, it's a thing. You're surfing online, when you hit the latest political controversy or catastrophic news story. It takes you to a negative place, but you can't stop. You follow the rabbit trail and binge on toxic thoughts about our country, the world, and everything going on around us. You know what I mean—we all lived through the dumpster fire that was 2020.

How about trying an experiment? Log out of your social-media accounts, personal email, and dating apps for a week and see what happens. You may discover they have been putting you on trains of thought leading in the opposite direction of peace.

Half Truths Are Half Lies

One of the biggest challenges about the anxious thoughts we have is that there is *some truth* in them. That's why they can be so powerful. If there was absolutely no truth to our thoughts, we wouldn't be tempted to dwell on them. But half truths are only half true, so they must be replaced with *full truths*. Stay with me if that sounds confusing. Some half truths could be:

- *I will never be good enough.*
- *I don't have friends who care about me.*
- *I will never get married.*
- *I am not pretty enough.*
- *I will never be able to conquer my depression.*
- *My brother will always be an addict.*
- *My mom is going to die from cancer.*
- *I may die in a car accident.*
- *My boyfriend is going to break up with me.*
- *I will never get promoted.*
- *I will never get out of debt.*

What makes thoughts like these hard to ignore is the little bit of truth in them. They are *partly* true but not the *whole* truth.

Maybe you think, *I may never get married.* There is some truth to that. You may never get married, but that isn't the full truth. God's Word states what is completely true: in Christ, you have everything you need. God will never leave you or forsake you. You have never been alone and never will be. You already have the only relationship that will truly satisfy.

You might find yourself thinking, *I will never be good enough.* That's partly true but not entirely. The entire truth is, you will never be good enough *on your own*. But the Bible says that through Christ you are *more* than enough. In fact, it says that when you feel weak (a.k.a. as if you are not enough), God's power is strong in you and makes you way more than enough. Shortcomings, according to the Bible, are superpowers because they can lead you to experience God's supernatural power.

Maybe you think, *I can't change*. That is partly true, because you can't change on your own. But Christ can change you and will change you if you surrender and walk with him. God can turn around and transform your life. You can leave your past in the past with his help.

Maybe you think, *My friends don't care about me*. I could tell you that of course your friends care about you, but that may not be true (especially if they're not Christians). What is true is that no matter who cares about you, we are here to care for people and serve, not be served. That's what we as Christians are on this planet to do: love people.

You might struggle with thinking that your value is found in how you look, where you work, or what you earn. Here's the truth: other people *can* determine your value by where you work, how much you earn, or how you look, but the opinions of other people don't matter and won't last. Your true worth has already been defined by God. He finds you so valuable that he gave his life for you. *That's* how much you are worth. What matters to the world does not matter to God. Are you going to let it matter to you? Will you let what others think define you, or let what Jesus did on the cross define you? That's a choice you have to make.

As I write this, we are in the middle of the COVID-19 pandemic, along with racial and political unrest. Hundreds of thousands of people in the United States have lost their lives, and millions of people have lost their livelihoods. Panic and fear have swept through homes. People have buried sons, daughters, mothers, fathers, grandparents, and friends.

It can be easy to think, *Someone I know could get this virus and die.*

I could get this virus and die!—which has some truth to it. You or someone you know could get sick and die. Or maybe you're worried that a friend will be a victim of police brutality. Some truth? Yes. But it's not the whole truth. The Bible says that God has numbered our days (see Job 14:5; Psalm 139:16). He is in control, and nothing happens without him allowing it. Before I was born, he had already determined the length of my life. I won't live one day longer or shorter than he has planned. That's the whole truth. I can rest in that or get on the Anxious Express. One road leads to peace, the other to panic.

Spider-Man

My son, Crew, is very much into superheroes right now. Spider-Man, Superman, Batman, Hulk, Captain America, Black Panther, and any other Avenger out there—he's here for it.

He changes his mind about who is his favorite every day, so he has a new superpower every day. It's either "Man, I can fly!" or he's shooting make-believe spiderwebs, doing a Hulk smash, or using some made-up superpower he's pretending he has. Because, you know, that's just what you do when you're four.

Crew's obsession with superpowers could be explained by the natural desire we all have to control the world around us: to save someone from dying, get the bad guy, protect ourselves, and make the world feel safe. We all feel the need to be in control. When circumstances make us afraid or anxious, we especially want to control them, so we commonly fall back on one particular phrase: "I struggle with control."

Think about that statement for a second. You're saying you struggle with something you've never had, don't possess currently, and will never have. You don't struggle with control; you struggle with *not* having control. Tolerating our anxiety because we "struggle with control" makes as much sense as my tolerating my son pushing over his little sister because he "struggles with super-Hulk strength." (Yes, he has actually said that.)

The truth is, you don't have control, but as a Christian, you know the One who does: God. He loves you and invites you to trust him. Or you can keep pretending you have control (and maybe faking like you have a superpower while you're at it).

Knowing the Trains

While we were in New York, we eventually made it to our destination to visit friends who live in the city. When we rode the subway with them, I noticed something: my friend, a New Yorker, never got on the wrong train. Why? Because he rides the subway every single day. He has familiarized himself with it. He could quickly point out what train to get on or not get on based on where we wanted to go.

Similarly, the more we rehearse and ingrain God's truth in our minds, the easier it becomes to get on the truth train when we're tempted to board the anxiety train.

This is part of what the Bible means in Romans 12:2 when it says we are to allow God's Word to transform us by the renewing of our minds. Change our thoughts, and we will change our lives. God told us that two thousand years ago, and today neuroscience confirms that this *is* how our minds work. As we repeatedly think thoughts, we create neural pathways in our brains that make it easier to think those same thoughts in the future. Just like a muscle, the more we use those neural pathways, the stronger they become.[3]

That's what makes it easy to continue thinking the same anxious thoughts we always have. But we can change that as we etch God's truth in our minds. The more we do, the less likely we are to get on the anxious train, and the more likely we are to get on the truth train. We want that, because the truth train will take us where we want to go.

7

It's About Perspective

Finding a Filter

Do you know the most popular Instagram filter? I know, I know. Who uses filters anymore? #NoFilter. Am I right? Well, if you have edited an Instagram post, you might have guessed people's favorite: the Clarendon filter. It beats out Gingham, Juno, Lark, Mayfair, Sierra, Valencia, and Walden.[1]

Why is Clarendon the most popular? I don't understand the science behind it, but I know the reason. Let's be honest, which filter do people put on their pictures? The one that makes them look best!

What other reason would we use a filter? We swipe through our options like they're potential matches on a dating app. *Not this one; it's unnatural. This one is so bright I look like I haven't seen the sun in a year. Vampire much? But this one . . . this one is just right. This will definitely get me some heart-eyes emojis in the comments.*

We want to look good in photos.

We've all had those moments when we're hanging out with friends and someone says, "We should take a group photo!" So you ask anyone you can find under the age of fifty to take the picture, and your friend sends it to you later that day. It's usually blurry, someone's eyes are closed, or maybe the wind caught your hair at just the right time to make it look like you just rolled out of bed. Whatever the photo looks like, you are stuck with it. The moment has passed. Your friends went home. You can't retake the picture. But even though you can't change what's in the picture, you *can* choose what filter you put on it.

In the same way, the apostle Paul would say you don't have a choice over what all is in the picture of your life, but you *do* have a choice over the filter you see it through. You don't decide the family you were born into, what skin color you have, what neighborhood you grow up in, or a million other aspects of your life story. But you *do* get to decide what filter you see it all through.

If you view everything through the filters of joy, gratitude, and eternity, you will experience more peace and less panic in your life. Let me say that again: a key aspect of combating anxiety is replacing your feelings of fear through cultivating the right emotions by seeing life through the right filters.

#1: Joy Filter

As Paul launched into how to battle anxiety, he started by saying,

> Rejoice [be joyful] in the Lord always. I will say it
> again: Rejoice! (Philippians 4:4)

This is another of those verses where I'm tempted to roll my eyes and think, *Are you saying we can just choose joy, Paul? It's that simple? Like, I just choose to be joyful? C'mon, man, how can you say that?* But remember, Paul wrote those words while chained in a prison cell, waiting to receive the death penalty. He clearly has the street cred to make such a claim.

Notice he doesn't say, "Rejoice in the circumstances." He says, "Rejoice *in the Lord*" in every circumstance. Paul would say you can choose to put the "joy in the Lord" filter over everything in your life.

What do I mean by "right" perspective? I mean with an *eternal* perspective. You can choose to see the world around you with either an *earthly* perspective, thinking, *Life sucks. This is always how it's going to be. Bad things always happen to me,* or you can choose to see the world with an *eternal* perspective, setting your eyes on the joy of spending an eternity in heaven with Jesus. *That's* how Paul was able to choose joy: he maintained an eternal perspective.

He repeatedly said things like, "The light and momentary pains are nothing compared to the eternity awaiting us" (see 2 Corinthians 4:17), and "To live is Christ and to die is gain" (Philippians 1:21).

His attitude was essentially, *No matter what I face, through Jesus I'm going to spend forever with God in paradise. A hundred years from now when I'm in heaven, the fact that I was chained to a prison guard for a few hard months won't be a big deal. I can always choose joy, no matter what, because my joy is in the Lord.*

So can you. You can choose joy too.

Whatever situation you're in, no matter how anxiety producing it may seem, you have an opportunity to reframe it with the "joy in the Lord" filter—to choose to see the goodness of God and find the positive in your situation. Before you run off, let me explain a little more.

Captive Audience

In his letter to the Philippians, Paul gives his own example of how he put on the joy filter. In the very first chapter of the book, he writes,

> I want you to know, brothers and sisters, that what has happened to me [my being thrown in prison] has actually served to advance the gospel. (1:12)

What? How can Paul being locked up advance the message of the gospel? He continues,

> As a result, it has become clear throughout the whole palace guard and to everyone else that I am in chains for Christ. And because of my chains, most of the brothers and sisters have become confident in the Lord and dare all the more to proclaim the gospel without fear. (verses 13-14)

How did the entire palace guard hear the gospel? The chains Paul mentioned were attached on one end to Paul's wrist and the other to a prison guard. The guards worked in shifts, so each day, Paul would have several guards attached to him.[2] Meaning he quite literally had a constantly rotating audience under lock and key. He had hours at a time to share Jesus with the prison guards. Maybe this is where the phrase "captive audience" came from. You can't get more captive than that.

Think about it. Most people in Paul's shoes would wonder, *Where's God now? How could he allow this to happen? Why won't he get me out of this prison? What is going to happen to me?* But Paul thought, *This is amazing. I have a chance every eight hours to share the gospel with someone new. Prison itself isn't ideal, but God is providing so many opportunities to honor him and save people.*

How could Paul think like this? In circumstances in which most people would be freaking out, he was filled with peace and a sense of his purpose. Why? Because he found his joy in the Lord. His happiness wasn't based on what was happening around him but rather in knowing Jesus and making him known.

He was able to look at his tough situation with the right perspective, which let him see God's goodness while locked up in prison. My guess is that someday in heaven, we will meet some of these Roman guards who put their faith in Christ after Paul shared the gospel with them. Imagine asking, "Who told you about Jesus?" and hearing them respond, "A prisoner named Paul, who I was chained to for eight hours."

Even in the worst, most mundane or frustrating moments, I can choose (and *must* choose) to look for how God is working and for his goodness. I can put the "joy in the Lord" filter on, whatever I'm facing. The more I do, the more my feelings shift from worry to joy.

#2: Thankful Filter

We've all heard the expression "Is the glass half-full or half-empty?" I am about to answer definitively, for all time, that age-old question. The answer might surprise you.

The response doesn't have anything to do with your wiring, how you were raised, or even how you see the world. It has everything to do with just one thing: Is the glass being emptied or is it being filled?

In other words, when you are emptying out a glass, you would say it's *half-empty*. But if you are filling it up, you would say it's *half-full*.

Yep. Mind. Blown.

Want to know what makes someone's life feel half-empty or half-full? It's a similar answer. Is he or she being constantly filled or constantly drained?

You know what leads to a half-empty life? Complaining. You know what I'm talking about. (We've all definitely been this person.) Complainers put a negative filter on their life's circumstances. Complainers master the ability to complain about anything. And when I say "anything," I mean *anything*.

The complainer driving down the road could be thankful: *Man, I'm so lucky. I have a car! This road is beautiful. I can't believe I live in a country like this—it's amazing!* But no, the complainer thinks, *Oh my goodness! No one knows how to drive! Please! What are you all doing?*

The complainer showing up at the office could think, *Wow! This is amazing! I have a job. So many people would kill for this job. I get paid to hang out with friends.* But more often, the complainer is muttering inside, *I hate my job. My boss is the worst. I am way underpaid, and everyone I work with is so dumb.*

Complainers think things like, *I wish I lived in San Diego. It would be seventy-two degrees year-round.* Do you know what they'd probably think if they lived in San Diego? *I wish I lived somewhere with seasons. Ugh, it's always seventy-two degrees in San Diego.*

Are you a complainer?

Maybe you complain to your friends about not being in a relationship: "I just want a relationship so bad. Why does everyone else have someone? Life is pointless without someone to share it with." Then you get in a relationship and all you talk about is how annoying your boyfriend (or girlfriend) can be, how you miss nights out with the guys (or girls), and how you just hope you get engaged soon.

The point is, some people are never satisfied and there is always something wrong. Why? Because they have mastered the art of complaining.

Their glass will always be half-empty because of the negative filters they put on everything.

Grateful Gains or Complaining Drains

Complaining isn't just something that drains our lives and makes things always seem half-empty; it's also something we are *commanded* not to do. Paul says,

> Do everything without complaining and arguing.
> (Philippians 2:14, NLT)

We are to do everything in life without ever complaining. "Everything, Paul? That feels a little aggressive." He would reply, "Yes, everything."

> Give thanks in all circumstances; for this is God's will for you in Christ Jesus. (1 Thessalonians 5:18)

God's will? Yep. If you have ever wondered about God's will for your life, this verse makes it clear that it *at least* includes being thankful.

Notice again it doesn't say to give thanks *for* every circumstance; it says to give thanks *in* every circumstance. Paul knew that whatever we face as Christians, we can always be thankful, knowing God is good and has promised to work everything together for good.

Just as you can complain about anything, you can also be grateful about anything. We can choose, and that choice leads to a "glass half-full" life.

Instead of being drained by complaining about how you hate your job, you can choose to be grateful that God has provided one for you. Instead of complaining about your coworker, you can choose to be grateful that God has put someone in your path to care for and share Jesus with. Instead of being angry as you sit in five o'clock traffic after work, you can choose to be grateful that you have a home to return to.

No matter what happens, you can say, "I am thankful." When you do, instead of your life draining from complaining, it will be gaining from gratefulness.

Study after study confirms what the Bible says: if you want to have joy in your life, express gratitude. One study found that practicing the habit of journaling for even just one minute a day what you are thankful for increases a person's general happiness the same amount as doubling his or her salary would.[3] In other words, it's not the happy-clappy, joyful people who are thankful; it's the thankful people who are joyful. No matter what life throws at them, they're still able to say, "God is good. God is at work. I choose to be thankful."

One remarkable example of this attitude is Matthew Henry, who was a pastor in England during the late 1600s and early 1700s. One day on his way home from work, he was robbed by a group of men who took all his money. What do you think his response was?

I know what mine would be: anger, bitterness, and wondering why God would allow the offense. I'm guessing most people's responses would probably be similar.

Henry went home and wrote in his journal,

> I thank you, God, that I have never been robbed before. Thank you that although they took my wallet, they didn't take my life. Thank you that although they took all that I had, all that I had was not very much. Thank you that it was I who was robbed and not I who did the robbing.[4]

Despite just having been robbed, Henry's "thankful" filter allowed him to thank God. In fact, he found four things for which he was thankful. After being robbed! How crazy does that seem? Talk about being thankful in every circumstance.

So, maybe you discover that your dishwasher is broken. Try saying to yourself, *All right, my dishwasher is broken. I guess I'll have more time to listen to a podcast or audiobook as I wash these dishes by hand.*

You might be sick, but your response could be, "God, thank you for sickness because it reminds me to be thankful for all the days I am healthy, which I tend to take for granted."

You didn't get the job you wanted? Instead of throwing a pity party (*I will never find a job; I'm such a failure*), you can try saying, "I'm grateful I had that opportunity, but it must not be God's best for my life, so thank you, Lord, for saving me from making the wrong career decision."

You cannot choose the things you face in life, but you *can* choose how you frame them. Just like with Instagram, you decide the filter you put on them. Use the wrong one—the negative, complaining filter—and your life won't look so great. Use the right one—the grateful, joyful filter—and your life will appear better than you imagined.

You can do that. You can be grateful, because God is good and because of what Christ has done.

#3: Eternal Filter

I know that some of the scenarios I've described aren't on the same level as what you may be walking through. A dishwasher being broken is one thing, but what about struggles like "My mom has brain cancer" or "I lost my job and haven't been able to find another one" or "My engagement fell apart"? What are you supposed to do then—put a thankful or joyful filter on it?

I am not saying to just smile and be positive. We've all walked through difficult times in the past or we will at some point. I've looked at my parents' divorce or my daughter's possible birth defects and thought, *I cannot see exactly what God is doing here.* I'm not smart enough to know how God is going to make good out of the most painful circumstances, but I am assured he is. He always is and always will. I know it's not necessarily easy to see or believe. It takes real effort and a surrendered heart to choose to trust God.

According to Ecclesiastes 3, God will make even the most painful moments in our lives beautiful. We will see *everything* made right. In Romans 8:28, Paul says something similar:

> We know that in all things God works for the good of those who love him, who have been called according to his purpose.

If you are a follower of Jesus, everything in your life is being shaped together to work for your good, even if you can't see how right now.

One thing that always reminds me of the way God works is football. Football? Let me explain. A while back, I got invited to a college football game at Texas A&M, my alma mater (Whoop!). Someone gave me tickets, and I got to sit in the second row, ground level. They were amazing seats. If you've ever seen a school football game (I really hope you have), the marching band comes out at halftime to perform a routine for the crowd.

That day, I learned that when you're watching the show from ground level, it looks like chaos. I was thinking, *What is going on right now? The tubas are about to run over the xylophones, the trombones have gone rogue, and the trumpets are spinning in circles. This looks like one big mess!*

In complete confusion, I looked up at the jumbotrons showing an aerial view of the field and realized, *Oh! They are spelling something out. It's all purposeful.* What looked chaotic and random on the ground was purposeful, beautiful, and woven together intentionally when *seen from above*. It looked so dysfunctional from my low perspective up close, but when you looked from a higher angle, there was purpose and intention.

I don't know what you're going through. I *do* know that if you're a believer, God has promised there will come a day when you're going to see it from above. You are going to see that God was using everything that seems chaotic, dysfunctional, and broken for your good. That truth alone should give you some peace of mind.

Depends on the Filter

Jesus comes to earth and lives a perfect life. He never sins. He spends his entire life pouring himself out for humanity. He gives sight to the blind, allows the lame to walk, heals the sick, and cleanses lepers. Everywhere he goes, he transforms people.

One day he's abandoned by all his friends and betrayed by one of them. He's taken before a crowd and wrongfully accused, and the crowd cries out, "Crucify this man!" (see Luke 23:21).

He's led away and crucified. He dies a brutal death at the hands of men he created and formed in their mothers' wombs. He's held up on a cross made of wood from a tree he shaped and gave life to. Now, *that's* a bad day. Well, it depends on how you frame it, because it was also the best day.

The greatest evil act in history—humanity killing their Creator—would also become the greatest act of love in all of history. It's not just the day Jesus died; it's the day *death* died. It's the day God opened up a doorway to life, saying, "I will provide a way. I will sacrifice myself so that anyone who trusts in me, instead of themselves, can have eternal life."

Wow.

It all depends on the filter you see it through.

Whatever onslaught of anxiety you are facing, you have been given the invitation to see things through the filter of joy in Christ, gratitude through the cross, and eternity on your mind. Change how you think, change how you see your circumstances, and you will change your life.

Part III
The Freaking Cherries On Top

8

Hide and Fear

Dealing with Shame

When God created the world, it was perfect and good (see Genesis 1:31). The crown of his creation was the first man and woman, Adam and Eve. They married in a ceremony performed by God, and the two became one flesh (see 2:23–24), which is the biblical description of what happens in marriage. The Bible says they were naked and without shame (verse 25).

Think about that. No shame. That means there was no insecurity about their bodies, no fear of what each other's spouse thought, no hiding from each other or God. Just two naked lovebirds running around the garden of delight (*Eden* means "delight") with their loving heavenly Father celebrating them.

God did not give them a list of laws or instructions. There was just one rule: *Don't eat from the tree of the knowledge of good and evil.* That's it. The entire Bible could fit on the little white paper inside a fortune cookie. Things were good.

Then it happened. Adam and Eve fell to the serpent's temptation, disobeying God's command, and everything in our world changed. Sin entered and brought with it death. It also brought shame and anxiety.

That day, Adam and Eve tasted more than just the forbidden fruit. After eating it, they felt shame for the first time. Shame led to an ambush by anxiety. They were confused, worried, and full of fear. Instead of enjoying God's presence, they felt a need to hide from him. They ran into the woods and sewed fig leaves together to cover their naked bodies. As Adam put it,

> I heard the sound of you [God] in the garden, and
> I was afraid, because I was naked, and I hid myself.
> (3:10, ESV)

Tragically, they hid their sin instead of bringing it to God for him to heal it. And humanity has allowed fear to push us into hiding our sin ever since.

As Adam and Eve hid, God started calling out, "Where are you?" (verse 9). God knows everything. He knew where they were. The question was not really a question; it was an invitation. He was calling them out of hiding so they could experience healing. God extends the invitation for healing to us today, but we need to come out of hiding to accept it.

Hiding Prevents Our Healing

What we conceal (or hide), God will not heal:

> Whoever conceals their sins does not prosper,
> but the one who confesses and renounces them
> finds mercy. (Proverbs 28:13)

I meet so many people who are still struggling with something they have done (or are still doing) or something that was done to them. They can't understand why it's still a problem. I tell them, "If you are hiding it, you are basically telling God that you don't want healing in that area of your life."

It might be an addiction to pornography, an eating disorder, overwhelming guilt from a decision in your past, an addiction to drugs or pain medication, guilt from lying about your résumé to get a job, or scars from your sexual history.

Whatever it is, if you hide it, it won't be healed. Not only that, but it will fester. Our secrets allow shame and guilt to settle in our hearts and invite anxiety to come along as well. Isn't that true? If you could somehow create a pie chart revealing the sources of your anxiety, how much of the pie would be taken up by shame and secrets from your past? Anxiety and shame have a long track record of going hand in hand.

Our shame leads to fear. Fear creates anxiety and we wonder, *What if other people knew? What would they think? What if they find out?* Hiding is a recipe not for peace but for shame, fear, and anxiety.

That's bad enough, but it gets worse. We have an enemy named Satan, who wants you to stay stuck in this bad place. He feeds you the lie "You can't tell anybody. If your secret comes out, your life will be over. You need to suffer in isolation, because if they knew the real you, they would reject you."

Satan whispers lies, but God is speaking truth into your life as he invites you to come out of hiding so you can experience the cure.

The Confession Cure

The cure happens when we come out of hiding. We find another example of the confession cure in James 5:16:

> Confess your sins to each other and pray for each other so that you may be healed.

James was one of Jesus's brothers. (Yes, Jesus had brothers. See Matthew 13:55 and Mark 6:3.) That had to be rough growing up! Imagine nine-year-old James getting reprimanded for getting into trouble with the neighborhood kids or talking back to his parents. Mary says, "Why can't you be more like your brother Jesus?"

"Because, Mom—news flash—he is God!"

It's hard enough to follow the typical rule-following firstborn child. But when he is *perfect*? That's *rough*.

But James didn't just see his brother's perfect dinner-table etiquette; he also witnessed Jesus supernaturally healing people. He saw him restore sight to the blind, give sanity to the insane, cleanse the skin of lepers, open the ears of the deaf, and heal the sick.

This same younger brother wrote, years later, that *you, too, can experience the healing of God* in your life. How? Through *confession* and *prayer.*

James said healing comes when you "confess your sins to each other" and then have those people pray for you. We also need to confess our sins to God, but an essential part of healing is confessing to some Christians how we have sinned and been sinned against. If you want to experience healing, you need to bring your secrets into the light through confession.

What Will They Think?

We often won't open up because we are terrified at being known. We wonder, *What would they think of me if they really knew?*

Let me tell you what they will think. They'll think you're really honest—that you're a lot like them, only more honest. We are all broken and on a journey. Beyoncé's lyric "I woke up like this" is not true. She did not wake up looking picture-perfect. No one does, because none of us is perfect.

Which means we can stop pretending to be.

If anyone is able to do this, it should be those of us who are Christians. Why? Because a requirement for becoming a Christian is admitting we are sinners in need of grace. You know how roller coasters have signs that say, "If you are not *this* tall, you cannot ride"? The sign God puts to become a follower of Christ says, "If you cannot admit you are a sinner, you cannot come in" (see 1 John 1:8–10). If we, the body of Christ, can't be open about our struggles, who can?

Tragically, too many Christians fail to accept God's invitation to open up to other believers about their struggles. This doesn't make them more holy; it makes them fake.

But the invitation from God to us all remains: if you want to experience recovery at a soul level, if you want to become all God intends, you have to tell someone where you are struggling.

You need to open up, whether it's to your church small group, a trusted friend who is a Christ follower, or a pastor at your church. When you do, when you finally share that you have a secret struggle, that person is going to think, *Me too. You're like me, only more honest. You really want to get well.*

God is saying to tell someone, to confess, because he loves you and wants you to experience healing. The choice is yours.

Healing Through Revealing

This principle about confessing—this path to freedom God gives us—changed my life in my early twenties, after I'd struggled from an early age. When I was in seventh grade, our youth group spent the night in a hotel on our way to a church camp. That night, another kid in our room turned the TV to a pornographic show.

That event led to my struggling with pornography for the next ten years. As I got older, porn became more common and easier to access. I found myself with an addiction I didn't want but couldn't quit.

I had a secret and I felt like I was drowning in shame. My secret and the shame of it led to fear. I was terrified of anyone finding out. Satan kept whispering, "If your secret comes out, your life is over." Anxiety *overwhelmed* me . . . for years.

Then, one day in college, a close friend of mine busted into my house and said, "I did it again. I looked at pornography, and I don't want to be this man anymore. Will you pray for me and ask me about how I am doing in this area going forward?" I was amazed. I had never seen someone be that honest.

I said, "Of course." I then confessed that I struggled with the same thing. We prayed and began to hold each other accountable. We installed software on our phones and computers so that anything we viewed on the internet was shown to each other and other guys in our small group. Through honest confession, prayer, and accountability, God began to bring healing and give us victory in our battles with pornography.

To this day, when I am tempted to (or actually do) lust after someone who is not my wife—whether on TV, Instagram, the internet, or out in public—I confess it to the guys in my small group and ask them to pray for me.

What is it that you would be most afraid to confess? More than likely it's *those things* you need to confess the most. When you do, you will begin to experience healing, less anxiety, and more peace.

The Dentist

When I was twenty-two, I went to the dentist for the first time. Yes, you read that right: the *first* time. I now understand this is bizarre, but back then I had no idea waiting so long was not normal. My mom had an "If it ain't broke, don't fix it" mentality, and my teeth were always pretty straight, so I never needed braces.

When I started my first job, I discovered I had dental insurance. I thought, *Dental insurance? What's that for? Wait, dentists? I think I've heard of that.* I decided, *Yeah, let's do this!* I had a vague notion that people hated going to the dentist, but it seemed new and exciting to me. So I went to see a dentist. I sat in that chair that leans back and had X-rays taken. Someone had told me you get a free toothbrush, so I was waiting for that and then thought I would be on my way.

After taking the X-rays, the dentist came in and said, "I have good news and bad news. The good news is you have pretty straight teeth. The bad news is you have fourteen cavities."

I was stunned. "Fourteen cavities? Do I even have fourteen teeth?" She said, "Yes, you do. But you can also have multiple cavities in one tooth. Several of your teeth have multiple cavities." At first I thought that might be kind of cool, as if a few of my teeth had accomplished something impressive, but I could tell from her disapproving look that I was mistaken.

She then began to ask a series of questions. "David, how often are you flossing? Do you actually even brush your teeth? How much soda are you drinking? Do you sleep with candy in your mouth?" I felt a little insulted but got the point: I wasn't flossing enough and needed to lay off the sweets.

She got busy drilling and filling each cavity. I left understanding why people hate going to the dentist.

When I opened my mouth earlier that day and allowed someone to look in for the first time, it helped me to address issues that were already there (fourteen cavities!) *and* take steps to stop further problems (fourteen more cavities!) from developing. I could have left and continued living as I had before (gargling with sugar water and not flossing), and I could have never again allowed a dentist to examine my teeth, but it would lead to consequences. In fact, things would only continue to get worse.

Just as we open our mouths to dentists to fix and prevent dental problems, we need to open our lives up to other Christians, allowing them to know where we are struggling and need help. If we refuse to do so, it will lead to consequences. We will continue in shame, fear, and anxiety. That is not the life God has for us. He wants to heal the areas of our hearts that are full of decay and bring life to them. But again, the choice is ours, because he doesn't heal what we won't reveal.

As you read this chapter, has something come to mind that you have never shared? Perhaps a secret you don't want to continue carrying, something you don't want to struggle with forever? It might be a problem with alcohol, an eating disorder, a battle with pornography or sexual sin, an addiction to medication, or a decision from the past that you feel shame about. Whatever it is, it causes you anxiety, and the thought of sharing it makes you even more anxious.

I get that, but if you will push through those fears and confess your secret to a small group or trusted friend in your life, you can begin to experience healing and freedom. God already paid for all your sins on the cross. Your sin does not define you, and it's time to move past it and leave it behind. Don't cover it; confess it.

What we reveal can heal, and we can move beyond anxiety to experience God's peace.

9

Cleaning Out the Closet

Dealing with Baggage

My wife and I love a good bingeworthy TV show. We have gotten hooked on shows like *24*, *Friday Night Lights*, *Lost*, *The Last Dance*, *Stranger Things*, *Gotham*, and *Blue Bloods*. A while ago, a friend told us there was a new show we had to see called *Tidying Up*.

You know how in *Hoarders* people keep everything? *Tidying Up* teaches you to get rid of things. A woman named Marie Kondo goes into people's homes and helps them get rid of anything cluttering their lives. I know, sounds riveting, right?

We were surprised by what we'll call her *approach*. Marie asks people to take out each item from their closets and examine it. The goal is to get rid of it. How do you do that? By talking about it and then doing it! You hold up each item and ask, "Does this spark joy?" and "Is this something that is part of my past, or something I want to bring into my future?" If you decide you can get rid of it, you tell it, "Thank you for being part of my life in a past season." Odd? Yes. Creepy? Maybe. Effective? The people on the show say yes.

We made it through only a few episodes, but we did get inspired to declutter. We began to go through our stuff and quickly discovered how many things we didn't even know we still had. We also realized we were holding on to items from the past that had no place in our future. Like what? Cargo shorts, pearl-snap shirts, out-ofstyle jeans, clothes we haven't been able to fit into since college, notes from people we dated in the past, old Kodak cameras, portable CD players (if you don't know, just google it), and so much more.

I even found a pair of binoculars I'd had since I was fifteen. I have *never* used them. Why have I kept them? *What if I take up bird watching someday? I'm going to need these!* I could not believe we were still holding on to so many things from our past.

What does this have to do with anxiety? Everything, actually. Think of your soul as having the closet of your life. Over time our "soul closet" can become cluttered with things from the past. Cluttered with what? As we go through life, we encounter disappointments, hurts, and suffering. Our wounds may be the result of sinful choices we make or of people sinning against us. Perhaps without even realizing it, we carry shame, pain, guilt, anger, hurt, fear, bitterness, embarrassment, and insecurity from our past into our future. Like Marie Kondo, God tells us to get rid of it:

> Get rid of all bitterness, rage and anger, brawling and slander, along with every form of malice. Be kind and compassionate to one another, forgiving each other, just as in Christ God forgave you. (Ephesians 4:31-32)

God says that if you're angry or bitter or hurt, you need to get rid of what you're holding on to. Until we decide to get rid of it, we are just continuing to bring it with us into our future, leading us to anxiety-filled lives we don't want to live.

I bet you have found an old shirt and thought, *I didn't realize I still had this shirt.* You never got rid of it, so it's been with you all these years.

That shirt isn't the only thing you have been carrying with you since your sophomore year of high school. Around the time you picked up that shirt, you also picked up a wound from a friend who betrayed you, or a hurt from your parents' divorce, or pain from some traumatic event.

Perhaps someone sexually abused you. It wasn't your fault. You were the victim of somebody's evil decision. That abuse changed your perspective on sexuality, the opposite gender, yourself, and maybe even God.

You may have struggled through the trauma of a sibling with a drug addiction, the suicide of a friend, your dad losing his job, or a friend lying about you.

Whatever it was, that tragic past experience played a role in shaping your life. It has also played a role in shaping your anxiety. Yes, your anxiety. Research shows that traumatic experiences produce anxiety in us and increase our likelihood of developing anxiety disorders.[1]

You need to get rid of it. If not, if you don't recover, you will keep carrying it with you into your future, and it will continue to shape who you become and what you feel.

But it doesn't have to. You can hold up what happened, ask, "Does this spark joy?" and decide that it was part of your life in a past season but that you are going to get rid of it. How? How do you clean out the closet of your soul and recover from the past? Let's figure that out.

Root Issues

I have a pecan tree in my backyard. For years, I hoped it would fill our lives with more pecans than we could handle. Candied pecans, pecan pies, pecan cookies, pecan . . . pizzas? But I was disappointed every year because the pecans wouldn't turn out the way I'd hoped. One year I had an arborist come look at it. (Yes, an arborist. As an adult, I have learned there are such things as arborists and dentists!) He told me that the problem with the tree was the roots. The roots were not getting enough water. If I wanted to grow pecans, I had to address the issue with the roots. He explained that what I *could* see above the ground was being shaped by what I *could not* see beneath the surface.

Our lives—what people see—are completely being shaped by what cannot be seen under the surface. Look at how God speaks of our "roots":

> See to it that no one falls short of the grace of God
> and that no bitter root grows up to cause trouble
> and defile many. (Hebrews 12:15)

What are bitter roots? They are hurts and resentments from our past. We store them in our "closets," and even though they are hidden from our sight, they influence everything. To experience peace in the future, we must recover from past hurts.

In fact, the Hebrews verse says that if we continue to let anger and bitterness take root in our hearts, it can "defile" us. Translation? *Resentment about something that happened yesterday will poison what is going to happen today.* Harboring bitterness toward people from the past will hurt your relationships with people in the future.

If you don't have peace in your heart, you will not have peace in your life.

Your ability to trust people, resolve conflicts, maintain friendships, have healthy dating relationships, and even have a future marriage will be affected by bitter roots beneath the surface.

Holding On to Hurts

As a pastor, I get to counsel couples I am going to marry. I always ask the groom- and bride-to-be, "Is there anyone in your life you haven't forgiven?"

The answer is usually yes. Sadly, so many of today's young adults grew up in homes where a parent was physically or emotionally absent or where their parents divorced, which is all incredibly painful. The people I counsel have often been wounded by others—parents, siblings, friends, a bully, or someone from a past dating relationship. It's common for me to find out they are holding on to hurt and bitterness.

I ask them to work through the process of forgiving whomever they are angry at *before* they get married. Then I tell them, gently but candidly, "I won't marry you until you do."

Why? It's not because I don't care about them; it's because I do. I love them and want to see them have healthy marriages.

I tell the people getting married, "If you can't learn to forgive someone who has deeply hurt you, you are not ready for marriage. Marriage is all about forgiving someone who deeply hurts you over and over and over again. If you are not able to do that, you are not prepared to step into marriage. By not forgiving, you have trained yourself to hold on to the hurt. If you haven't forgiven, what makes you think you're the type of person who will forgive your spouse?"

It's almost always the case that when someone is still bitter, the person he or she has not forgiven is from some intimate relationship. It's usually a father or mother, a sibling, or some other family member. That's why the pain is so deep. I tell the person, as lovingly as I can, "You will have the same experience with your spouse. You are going to be hurt, sometimes intentionally and sometimes unintentionally. It's part of being married to a sinful human being. You will be hurt, and you will have to forgive. That's why *if you have not forgiven someone, you are not ready to get married.*"

I also explain to the couple, "If you have bitter roots under the surface, you are planting this marriage in bad soil. You may not see the roots, but they've been shaping your life and will shape your marriage. You need to get rid of them. It's time to forgive so you can move into a free future together."

Bitter Roots Are Growing

Now is the time—whether you're single, dating, or married—to form a habit of forgiving. If you have bitter roots below the surface, they will continue to grow and have an effect on what's above the surface, attacking you with anxiety, robbing you of peace, and breaking down your relationships.

So, before we continue, use these "what lies beneath" questions to help you identify whether you have any roots of bitterness growing:

- Is there anyone part of you hopes will fail in some way or you would like to see suffer?
- Is there anyone whose name, when it's brought up, makes you angry or resentful?

- Is there anyone you'd avoid in public because of something that happened between you?
- Is there anyone you are unwilling to let back into your life until he or she apologizes?
- Is there anyone you haven't forgiven?

If you answered yes to any of the above, you have a root of bitterness growing in you beneath the surface. You need to get rid of it because, even though you can't see it, it is dangerous.

Buried Bombs

During World War II, American and British air forces dropped thousands of bombs all over Germany to weaken the Nazi war machine. Though most of them exploded, thousands did not. They landed and submerged into the muddy German terrain, never exploding. They are still there, and every now and then, someone will find one.[2]

A construction crew will come in, begin to dig to clear land for a new building or housing project, and find a bomb. They evacuate the entire city or town around it as they try to defuse the bomb. If they can't defuse it, they have to set it off. Why? Because it's an ever-present danger; the bomb may not go off today, but it could explode at any time.

If you hold on to anger from past hurts, it's like a bomb buried beneath the surface, always at risk of exploding. It may not happen today, but as long as it remains buried beneath the surface, it is a danger to you and every person around you.

Can you imagine living in a city where you know bombs are buried? You would be anxious! You could never have real peace of mind. In the same way, instead of peace, you will have anxiety when your heart has anger lodged inside.

So, the question is, *How do you defuse the bombs of past hurts?* You have to get rid of them. The Bible says getting rid of them happens through the process of forgiveness, and forgiving is all about releasing.

Release the Debt

To recover from past hurts, we must release the anger and bitterness. We do this through forgiveness:

> Bear with each other and forgive one another if any of you has a grievance [holds a grudge] against someone. Forgive as the Lord forgave you. (Colossians 3:13)

What is forgiveness? It is releasing our right to retaliate against someone who hurt us. It's releasing justice to God for the wrong done to us. When we forgive, we are, in effect, saying, *God, I choose not to hold what they did against them. I release my desire for justice to you.*

Why would we do that? One reason is that, as Christians, we know that every sin committed against us will be paid for, either by the person's suffering in hell for all eternity or on the cross by Jesus.

Another reason we forgive is because it sets us free. We often think that by forgiving, we release the other person from responsibility. But *we* are released and can finally experience freedom from the hurts that have held us back and hindered our relationships.

If you want a life marked by peace instead of anxiety, you need to forgive.

But we balk at the idea of forgiveness. I think part of the reason we don't want to forgive is that we don't understand forgiveness. So let's cover what it's not.

Forgiveness is not forgetting. You can't forget. Our brains don't work that way. In order to forgive someone, you don't have to pretend it never happened.

Forgiving is not excusing sin. What happened *is* wrong, *does* hurt, and *should* make you angry. Sin makes *God* angry and grieves his heart. God tells us, "Do not repay anyone evil for evil" (Romans 12:17). He calls what happened to you "evil."

Forgiveness is not pretending it didn't happen. It's not saying, *Oh, it never hurt. I'm fine. Everything is good.* When we forgive, we acknowledge our hurt but still choose not to hold on to bitterness against others.

Forgiveness is not conditional. Often people think, *If he comes and begs for my forgiveness, then I'll give it to him, but not until then.* Forgiveness is commanded; it is not conditional (see Matthew 18:21–22). Jesus forgave those who crucified him *while* he was being crucified. He didn't place requirements before extending forgiveness, and neither should his followers. Remember, while you wait for someone to come apologize, you are holding on to a hurt that is only going to hold you back from recovering and from the life God has for you.

Forgiveness is not any of that. Forgiveness is saying, *What you did was wrong. I hurt and I am not excusing that sin. But I am choosing not to hold it against you. I'm releasing that to God. I'll trust him with whatever vengeance or restitution needs to take place. That's ultimately in his hands, not mine. I am going to let it go.*

Raccoon Traps

I was talking to a friend who grew up on a farm out in the country . . . like the *super* country. He told me raccoons would come try to kill his chickens. To prevent this, he set up traps. The traps were not what you might imagine. He would drill a small hole into the side of a log and put a shiny object, like a piece of aluminum foil, in it.

Raccoons would come reach their paw in to grab the shiny object. The hole was big enough to fit in their unclenched fist, but when they clenched the object and made a fist, they couldn't get their paw out.

At any point, they could just release the shiny object and be free, but they refused to let go. They were trapped, not realizing they could be free if they would just let go.

In the same way, God wants you to be free—but as long as you hold on to hurts, you are trapped. By refusing to forgive, you continue to hold on to the shiny object. You don't have to. God invites all of us to release our hurts to him and forgive others as we have been forgiven.

Canceled Debt

The disciples heard Jesus talk about forgiveness *a lot*. Peter once asked Jesus to elaborate. He asked, "Jesus, how many times do I forgive someone who sins against me?" Peter then added, I bet with some pride, "Up to seven times?" (see Matthew 18:21). That suggestion would have made himself feel good, because no rabbi taught to forgive that much. Peter was like, "Hey, look how generous I am. Up to seven times? Hey! How about that? Look how great I am."

Jesus responded, "Not seven times, Peter. Seventy times seven!" (see verse 22, NLT).

Then jaws dropped open all around Jesus. They understood he was teaching that you never stop forgiving.

Why do we never stop forgiving? Because God doesn't stop forgiving us. Jesus explained with a parable (see verses 23–35). He said, with my modernizing the story just a bit,

> The kingdom of heaven is like this. There is a guy, we'll call him Joe, who has a six-billion-dollar debt.
>
> One day a rich lender says to Joe, "You are overdue on your debt. It's time to pay."
>
> Joe responds, "I can't. It's six billion dollars!"
>
> The lender says to his henchmen, "All right. Take Joe, everything he owns, and his family, and sell it all. We'll take whatever we can make from the sale."
>
> Joe throws himself to his knees and begins to beg. "I'll pay it back. Please give me enough time. Please show me mercy."

Pay back six billion dollars? Everyone listening to the story knew Joe could never pay it. Jesus continued:

> The lender decides to show mercy and cancel Joe's debt.

(Whoa. That's a good day. I mean, finally paying off your student loans is an amazing feeling. When you get six billion paid off, that's a pretty exciting day.) Jesus went on:

> On his way home, Joe bumps into some dude, Bill, who owes him a thousand dollars.
>
> Joe grabs Bill and says, "Where's my money?"
>
> Bill begs, using the same words Joe had just used himself: "I'll pay it back. Please give me enough time. Please show me mercy."
>
> But Joe says no and has Bill thrown in jail.

(Wow!) Jesus then explained,

> The rich lender, the one who forgave Joe's six-billion-dollar debt, finds out what happened. So he goes to Joe and tells him, "You wicked servant. I forgave you a million times more than what he owed you. I forgave a debt you could never pay back. This dude Bill actually could pay back what he owed you, yet you didn't show mercy to him?" And the lender has Joe thrown in jail until his original six billion dollars is paid off.

(I'm pretty sure that would take . . . forever.) Jesus finished the story by saying,

> This is how my heavenly Father will treat each of you unless you forgive your brother or sister from your heart.

Jesus's point was, whatever someone did to you, as evil and hurtful as it might be, it pales in comparison to what you have done to God. He chose to forgive you, and you must choose to forgive.

As Joe should have done in the story, you look at the person who hurt you and say, "I am canceling the debt. You don't owe me anymore."

You Don't Owe Me Anymore

My parents got a divorce when I was twelve years old. My siblings and I ended up living with my mom and seeing my dad only a couple of times a month. It felt normal at the time, but I later realized I was carrying a lot of hurt and resentment toward him. Later, I began to process the pain. I understood that the Bible said I had to cancel the debt, but I was struggling a bit in knowing how. Then some mature Christians told me, "It's really hard to cancel a debt if you don't know *what* the debt is. You need to identify what was taken. Then you can decide to cancel it."

I sat down and began to write out very specifically what was taken from me:

> You took from me having a father around. You took from me having a dad come to my games and root for me in high school and college. You took from me the safety I should have felt growing up, because on Monday nights I had to drive across town to that terrible apartment. You took from me having an example in my life of what it looks like to love a wife.

I put it all down, and then I wrote, "I'm deciding you don't owe me anymore." I didn't need to show it to him; I needed to identify the debt for me so I could cancel the debt.

My heart breaks knowing you're carrying pain from what's happened to you. I don't know what was taken from you. Maybe it was . . .

- your virginity
- having a mother who loved you the way a mom should

- having a father to love you and show you how to be a godly man
- shame-free years because of an abortion he said you had to have
- being able to look in the mirror and feel good about yourself
- Christmases with both parents in the same home

I get it, and I am so sorry. But if you want peace in your future, you cannot hold on to hurts from your past. You have to let them go. One of the healthiest things you can do is sit down and write out the following:

> This is what was taken from me _____, and I am deciding to cancel the debt by giving forgiveness.

By doing so, you are deciding not to allow your past to rule your future.

Future You

Remember *Tidying Up*, the show about decluttering your life? I love the clarifying question she tells people to ask about the things they find in their closets: "Is this something I envision taking into my future with me?" In other words, Is this something I want as part of my future life, or something I should leave in the past?

Are these Birkenstock sandals something I want to be part of my future, or are they better left in my past? Pretty clarifying! Sorry, Birks, you are not coming into the future with me.

You probably have hurts you've been holding on to for which you need to ask, *Is this something I envision taking into the future with me, or if I want to live a life full of peace and free of anxiety, is it better left in my past?*

For example, perhaps someone sexually abused you. It was not okay, and it was not your fault. It is understandable that you carry immense hurt and you struggle to trust people. Let's say you are twenty-four and we roll the clock forward sixteen years to when you're forty. Your family throws an over-the-hill party for you. You are surrounded by the most important people in your life. Picture yourself sitting there surrounded by loved ones. Do you want that person (you) to still be ashamed, angry, and afraid?

I bet you don't. If that's true, if you want to be free in the future, you can choose to recover from what happened. With God, you can begin working through the process of forgiving the people who have sinned against you. You have a God who loves you and is saying to you, "You can trust me with that. Every sin will be paid for on the cross for all eternity. Give that to me. Don't hold on to hurts that will only hold you back. It doesn't spark joy, and it's time to get rid of it."

By making the decision today to let go of pain in your past, you can and will experience more peace in the future.

10

The Obstacle Course

Dealing with Stress

I was a Division 1 (the highest possible level) college athlete. (Shocking, right?) How? I didn't play baseball or football. I threw the javelin. I counted and I think there are about three people on the planet who throw javelin. That explains how I was able to do it at a D1 school.

Javelin is a track-and-field event, which is a spring sport, so the fall season is filled with nothing but strength and conditioning. Our two-time Olympian coach, Chico, created various strength tests to evaluate how we had grown through each semester. The most notorious physical test, because it was the most grueling, was known as the obstacle course. Throughout freshman year, my older teammates told me how excruciating the test was. It sounded as though they were describing a root-canal surgery with no anesthesia.

When the day finally came for the obstacle course, I still didn't know exactly what to expect. I felt an odd mixture of insecurity and pride. My thoughts ranged from *Am I about to die?* to *I'll crush this and probably set a new record.*

What was the obstacle course? The coach timed you as you carried a sixteen-pound metal weight while running through an obstacle course, jumping over hurdles, then running up and down the aisles of the stadium bleachers. And when you completed the course?

You did it all over again! If that doesn't sound miserable enough, we had to run the course with our whole team watching.

As we all stood waiting to be tortured, our coach looked at me and said, "Hey, you're the youngest. You go first. Set the pace." *Awesome.* I stepped up to the line. My coach shouted, "Ready, set, go!" and I took off, picked up the sixteen-pound weight, ran as fast as I could, jumped over hurdles, and raced up and down the bleachers. I got to the top of the last aisle, finishing lap one, set the weight down, picked up the second weight, and started lap two.

I was feeling amazing and thinking, *I am a phenom! Maybe I should try out for the Olympics!* Out of the corner of my eye, I glanced at my coach and saw him showing another coach my time. Clearly, he was as surprised as I was. *Yes!* Then I got to the first bleacher to run up and down the aisles and realized, *Houston, we have a problem.* Suddenly my body said, *Shut 'er down!*

The technical explanation for what happened is that lactic acid filled my legs. That happens when there's not enough oxygen in your muscles. I didn't understand the metabolic reaction happening inside me. I didn't know my body contained that much acid or lacked that much oxygen. I just knew that I could no longer run. My all-out sprint turned into a defeated limp. I went up and then down the stairs like an elderly woman with two artificial hips and extreme arthritis in both knees.

The leg cramps and fatigue were only second to my embarrassment of the entire track team watching it happen. What had occurred was so pathetic that they weren't mocking me; they were looking at me in horror mixed with sympathy. I could almost hear their thoughts: *Someone please make this stop. Look at him. How is it possible for someone to be so unathletic? I think my grandma could beat him in a fight.*

Finally, I got to the very end and collapsed.

My coach came over and said, "David, that was the fastest first lap I have ever seen . . . and that was the slowest second lap I have ever seen."

Thanks, Coach.

What happened? My pace caught up to me, and my pace *cost* me.

Doesn't that often happen to us in life? We run at an unsustainable pace. Our busyness leads to our feeling mentally, emotionally, spiritually, and physically exhausted. The unsustainable pace is overwhelming but seems unavoidable. In fact, we feel pressure to do more—make more money, work more, exercise more, make more friends, go on more dates, eat healthy more often, save more, pay off more debt, and somehow sleep more. We have to do more! We can't do less.

Our faith often feels the same way. We put expectations on ourselves—that we should be praying more, reading the Bible more, giving more, attending church more, and serving more.

What does this unsustainable pace and drive to do more lead to? Anxiety, stress, and feeling overwhelmed.

Maxed Out

If you ask the average young adult, "How are you doing?" you are likely to hear some version of "I'm good, just really *busy*" or "I'm okay; I just have *a lot* going on."

What's interesting is that the feeling of being overwhelmed is not just *tolerated;* it's almost *celebrated*. It can feel like we're in a competition of who is the busiest and most stressed out.

What if you asked someone how he's doing and he responded, "Doing good; I'm enjoying life as I move at a slower pace," or she said, "Things are going well; I'm working sustainable hours at the office and have healthy work-life boundaries, so I'm rarely stressed"? What would you think? Probably, *What's wrong with him? He clearly has no drive.* Or, *Wow, I never realized she's lazy.*

This "feeling overwhelmed because overworking is cool!" mentality is built into the fabric of our society. If resting were an Olympic sport, the USA would not be taking home any medals. According to the International Labour Organization, "Americans work 137 more hours per year than Japanese workers, 260 more hours per year than British workers, and 499 more hours per year than French workers."[1]

One study found that in the United States, a majority of salaried employees work an average of *more than* forty hours a week.[2] The results of overworking can be crippling. A six-year study of 2,123 workers found that those who worked at least eleven hours per day were two and a half times more likely to become depressed than those who worked seven or eight hours per day.[3]

Not only do Americans work more hours, but we also take less time off for vacation.[4] Even when we do take vacation time, the stress of life and work follows us, thanks to technology. Author Daniel H. Pink, in an article in the *New York Times,* explained that our smartphones and computers ensure we are never really "away"— that vacation "used to be like an on-off switch" but now, because of technology, it's become "more of a dimmer switch."[5]

No wonder everyone is so anxious!

Stressed Out

Want to hear something crazy? For most of history, the English word *stress* was primarily a term associated with physics or science. For example, if a metal beam begins to bend from weight or force, it's under stress. Stress means that the beam's limit has been reached and the applied force is about to break it. Only in the past few decades have people started using the term *stressed* to describe a feeling experienced internally by a person and not physically by an object.[6]

How did *stressed* become a term applied to people? I don't know, but I picture someone at a construction project seeing a metal beam about to break and thinking, *I feel like that is my life. I am like that metal beam being crushed by weight under stress.* Maybe that's not how it happened, but it doesn't really matter. Society started applying this term meaning "at the limit and about to break" to describe people's lives, and it caught on . . . *fast.*

People can be financially, emotionally, professionally, mentally, relationally, and even spiritually stressed. We constantly feel overwhelmed by life's demands and unable to keep up. This adds to our anxiety and steals our peace. But what if we don't have to live that way?

Sister, Sister

If you grew up in the nineties, you know about *Saved by the Bell*, boy bands, *Super Mario World*, the Sony Walkman, "It's morphin' time," *Captain Planet and the Planeteers*, Blockbuster Friday nights, and the rich kid who actually had a computer *in his house*. You also know *Sister, Sister*. This TV show starred Tia and Tamera as identical twins who were separated at birth but magically meet as teenagers in a clothing store. What do they do? They each convince their adoptive single parents to move in together, of course!

What does that have to do with anything? Not much, but every time I read about the sisters Mary and Martha in the Bible, I can't help but think about *Sister, Sister*. Call it part of the curse of growing up in the nineties.

In Luke 10, Mary and Martha have Jesus over to their house, and their interaction with him shows the danger behind the maxed-out mindset so common in our world today:

> Jesus entered a village. And a woman named Martha welcomed him into her house. And she had a sister called Mary, who sat at the Lord's feet and listened to his teaching. But Martha was distracted with much serving. (verses 38–40, ESV)

Jesus comes strolling into her hometown, so Martha invites him and the disciples over to hang at her place. That's when Jesus begins teaching the disciples, right there in Martha and Mary's living room. Can you imagine? How cool would it be to have Jesus teaching in your house?

Martha goes into full panic mode: *Jesus is at my house! What should I serve him? What do you serve the Son of God for lunch? Maybe some fish? No, that feels so cliché. Plus, I only have one fish, and there are*

thirteen of them! Of course, he did do that whole multiply-the-fish trick.
Maybe that's easy for him. I could just say, "Jesus, here's a fish. Do your
thing!" No, that would be disrespectful. What do I make for lunch? If only
I had some Hot Pockets or Lunchables!

Martha is figuring out what to feed her guests and getting the
food together, but Mary slips out of the kitchen and into the living
room to listen to Jesus teach. Martha realizes her sister has left her
all alone to put lunch together and decides to do something about it:

> She went up to him [Jesus] and said, "Lord, do you
> not care that my sister has left me to serve alone?
> Tell her then to help me." (verse 40, ESV)

Basically, Martha says to Jesus, "What's the deal? My sister in
here is acting like a hippie, sitting at your feet. Ain't nobody got time
for that! I need help in the kitchen. Tell her to help me!" I feel for
Martha. She is working alone in the kitchen, trying to be a good
host. Shouldn't Mary be in there helping her?

There's a lot to respect about Martha. She seems to be the responsible one. She owns the home. She's paying the bills. She appears to have drive and ambition. She is a go-getter, caring for the
needs of others. Martha seems like the most eligible single girl in
town! If ABC and Chris Harrison were around back then, I'm sure
she would have been first pick for *The Bachelorette*.

Mary, on the other hand, seems to be a freeloader, hanging in her
sister's living room, mooching off others' hard work. Who *does* that?

Like me, Jesus also feels for Martha, but not because she doesn't
have enough help in the kitchen. Jesus knows that is not her biggest
problem. He recognizes she has an issue far more important than
whatever she is making for lunch. Jesus looks at her and says,

> Martha, Martha, you are anxious and troubled
> about many things, but one thing is necessary.
> Mary has chosen the good portion, which will not
> be taken away from her. (verses 41-42, ESV)

Martha had a full to-do list of cooking, preparing, and serving, and she ended up maxed out, stressed out, and missing out on the one thing that was most important: Jesus. She traded sitting with the Prince of Peace for a kitchen full of platters and a heart full of panic.

In the story, Martha is described as *distracted, anxious,* and *troubled*—three words that accurately describe many of our lives. These three words connect to each other. Being distracted makes us anxious. To be troubled—by things in the past or future—makes us distracted. If you are anxious, you are troubled. If you are distracted from the present by something you are anxious about in the past or future, you will feel troubled.

Death by Distraction

The origin of the word *distracted* comes from a French word for "torture." If the French really wanted to torture someone, they would distract them. They would tie ropes to the person's legs and arms, then tie the other end to horses, who would run in every direction and pull the person apart. The result was called "death by distraction."[7]

That may not sound like the kind of distraction we're familiar with, but it's weirdly similar. We know what it feels like to be pulled in many directions at the same time. Distraction today won't literally kill you, but it can kill the best of you. It robs you of your ability to be present in the moment, invest in relationships, rest, focus, and enjoy life.

Distraction drives our busyness, and it's a major cause of anxiousness and stress. It often leads to us feeling maxed out and overwhelmed. And as we saw with Martha, when you are maxed out, you can miss out on what's most important.

Guess Who's Coming to Dinner?

If you could choose to have anyone in history over for dinner, who would you choose? Maybe you would choose Martin Luther King

Jr., Mother Teresa, Martin Luther, Abraham Lincoln, Justin Bieber, or Beyoncé. No judgment here. You do you.

Can you imagine if that person came to your house and you spent the whole time upstairs vacuuming and cleaning? How dumb would that be?

That is exactly what happened that day in Martha's home. She invited Jesus into her home. She had the Son of God in her living room. There is no more important person in all of human history, and he was sitting on her couch. What did Martha do? Did she spend time with him? No. She was in the kitchen cooking and cleaning.

What happened to Martha often happens to us. We invite Jesus into our lives. We have him living inside us. Yet we, too, are tempted constantly by distractions that take our focus away from Jesus.

The distractions—our jobs, relationship statuses, weekend plans, finances, health, families, friends, social media—are not bad things, and they matter. But even still, they pull our attention away from what matters most.

We live distracted, we neglect what is most important, and it makes us feel *anxious*.

Hours in the Day

There are just not enough hours in the day. You've probably said it. I wonder how many hours of my days I've wasted saying it. Our work demands, and everyday responsibilities, and doctor's appointments, and social lives, and church activities, and spiritual health, and time with family, and never-ending to-do lists require more time than we have to give.

We wake up every day with the goal of accomplishing as much as possible, but we rarely make it through our lists. We add whatever is left over to tomorrow's list of things to get done. Our lists get longer and longer. Life can feel like running on a treadmill that is simply moving too fast.

The truth is that life moves at the same pace for all of us. We all get 24 hours in our day, 7 days in our week, and 365 days in our year.

That's the allotted time for me, for you, and even for Beyoncé. So what's the problem? It's not that *life* is moving faster but that *we* are moving too fast for life. We're simply trying to do too much.

Resist Maxing Out

Think about it this way. Let's say that tomorrow you head over to your local gym and get on a treadmill. You hit start. The machine automatically takes you to the pace of five miles per hour. It's a light jog, so you decide to increase the speed. But when you do, you realize there's only one speed. In fact, all the treadmills are set to the same speed. You think, *I should change gyms. This is not that challenging at all.*

You are moving along at five miles per hour, when a line forms with people asking you to carry things for them as you jog. Your girlfriend hands you a *box of chocolates* representing your *love life.* Easy. You continue jogging with the box. Your boss comes up and hands you a *computer* representing *your job.* You think, *No problem. I can handle this.* Your pastor walks up and hands you a *Bible* representing your *spiritual growth.* Then your roommate hands you a *dog leash* representing *the dog you decided to get* after you graduated from college. Then another friend hands you a *personalized leather journal* representing the *side hustle* you started on Etsy. Someone else hands you a bottle of *Topo Chico* representing your *social life.*

You continue running, now carrying the box of chocolates, computer, Bible, dog leash, journal, and Topo Chico. Jogging has become difficult, and you almost drop one or two items but still think to yourself, *I've got this.* As you do, your mom comes up and hands you a *framed picture,* which represents *your family* and how *she would sure like to see you more.* Your doctor comes right behind her and hands you a *dumbbell* representing your need to *exercise regularly to be healthy.* Finally, your friend shows up and hands you a *phone* representing your *social media,* which by the way, is not nearly as active as it should be and doesn't have enough followers.

Do you feel stressed out yet?

Well, here comes someone from the IRS, cable company, Wi-Fi

network, apartment leasing office, student loan company, and credit card company. Each hands you an envelope with an invoice in it. As you reach to take the envelopes, the juggling act you've been trying to pull off—not to mention the unbearable weight of it all—hits a breaking point and you drop *everything*.

What was the problem? It was not the fixed pace of the treadmill; it was the amount you tried to carry while on it. Similarly, our problem is *not* the pace of life, which is fixed; our problem is the amount we are trying to carry.

Right Amount on the Right Things

Reducing stress involves resisting the urge to max out your time and restricting what you allow to fill your life. In other words, it's not just spending your time and energy on the *right number* of things but on the *right things*.

What good is it if you keep running on the treadmill of life but miss the point of life itself? Sure, you were able to balance spin class three times a week, multiple social-media accounts, a full-time job, your side hustle, and caring for your Yorkie, but you didn't grow in your relationship with God, have healthy relationships, or experience peace.

The question is not "How much can I do each day?" but "*What* should I do each day?" If you want a life full of purpose and peace instead of stress and anxiety, you must learn to resist the temptation to do it all.

WWJHMD

When I was growing up, bracelets with the letters WWJD were huge. WWJD stood for "What would Jesus do?" Wearing the bracelet would hopefully remind you to think through the lens of "If Jesus were here, what would he do?"

Great idea, but I think there's an even better question Christians should ask: "What would Jesus *have me* do?" Yep, WWJHMD. The bracelets wouldn't look nearly as cool, but that question provides a better filter.

Why? Because sometimes what Jesus would do is not what he would have you do.

For instance, let's say you discover that your coworker forgot to bring his lunch to work. WWJD? If Jesus were there, he might take your fish sandwich and miraculously turn it into twenty sandwiches or into one of those giant six-foot subs so he could feed the whole office. He could do that because he is God.

Is that what he would *have you* do? No. He would have you give your coworker half your sandwich.

Focusing on what Jesus would have you do can help you eliminate distractions and stress. Rather than coming up with a list of all that you need to do today, focus on *What would Jesus have me do today?* Getting every single thing you want done is not usually possible. Prioritizing what God wants you to do is always possible.

But what if you're not sure what priorities God says are most important? Don't worry; I've got you covered. One day, some guy asked Jesus to tell him the most important command in the Bible. It's a similar question to the one I've proposed: *What does God want me to do today?* Here is Jesus's response:

> "Love the Lord your God with all your heart and with all your soul and with all your mind." This is the first and greatest commandment. And the second is like it: "Love your neighbor as yourself." All the Law and the Prophets hang on these two commandments. (Matthew 22:37–40)

Love God and love people. *That's* what God wants you to focus on today. If your schedule keeps you from doing that, you are not just *maxed out;* you are *missing out.*

Resist Missing Out

Mary sat at Jesus's feet, hanging on every word. Martha stood in the kitchen, chopping celery and pouring lemonade. Jesus said, "Mary has chosen the good portion" (Luke 10:42, ESV). The phrase *good portion* was a food analogy. It's almost like Jesus said, "Mary chose the filet mignon."

What was the better portion she received? It was being with Jesus, knowing him, learning from him, and deepening her relationship with him.

We can also choose the better portion. How? By choosing to spend time reading the Bible and talking to God in prayer. You can start tomorrow morning. Wake up and spend twenty minutes with him. If you're not sure where to start, read a chapter from one of the four gospels. Write down one thing that stands out to you. Then pray, telling God what you are anxious about and asking him for help.

If that sounds like too much, start with five minutes.

Is that all that it means to love God? No, of course not.

But starting with the Bible and prayer is a great way to connect with God and prepare yourself for a day of *What would Jesus have me do?*

Resist Relying on Yourself

Want to hear something crazy? You know that famous miracle where Jesus took a couple of fish and pieces of bread from some kid's lunch box and fed like five thousand people? That miracle happened in the chapter right before the story where Jesus went to Martha's house.

Think about that! I bet Martha *wanted* to be in listening to Jesus. She just felt like she couldn't. Why? Because she had thirteen guests at her house, including *the Son of God,* and she had to figure out how to feed all of them.

What if, instead of freaking out about all that had to be done, Martha went to Jesus and told him exactly what she was feeling? "Jesus, I'm worried about the food. I don't want to be that person, but I don't have enough here for you all to eat. Honestly, it's got me overwhelmed with anxiety. But I know that like a week ago you took a little bread and fish and fed five thousand people. So, well, I'm pretty sure you can handle the whole food situation. I am choosing to rely on you for this problem instead of being stressed out about it."

That day could have been completely different for Martha. Rather than relying on her ability to provide for Jesus, she could have relied on Jesus's ability to provide for her.

Sadly, that didn't happen. Martha's self-reliance kept her busy working and worrying. She was too busy to spend time with Jesus. Her busyness pushed her away from not only Jesus but also peace.

Your life can be completely different. Jesus cares about you, doesn't want you to be anxious, and invites you to come to him for help. Rather than relying on your ability and doing everything you can, rely on Jesus's ability and do what he would have you do.

Part IV

Where We Freak Out

II

Flipping Golf Carts

Romantic Anxiety

I have an unconventional hobby called flipping golf carts. I don't mean that I flip golf carts by driving them recklessly. I also don't mean that I run up and push over golf carts like you do to cows when cow tipping. I mean that I *flip* golf carts—think Chip Gaines on *Fixer Upper*. Instead of houses, I flip golf carts. I keep a lookout on Craigslist, Facebook Marketplace, and resale apps. I find a golf cart to buy, fix it up, and sell it to make some money. (My primary goal is to *not lose* money.)

Recently, I found a cart about an hour outside Dallas. Thankfully, Kevin, the seller, accepted my offer, so I rented a trailer and went to pick the golf cart up. When I pulled up to the house, I met the owner of the cart. Kevin lived in a fascinating neighborhood: a gated community of twelve homes, each with a five-acre plot of land. The coolest feature? The airstrip, where small planes could land in the middle of the community.

Kevin's massive property was clearly taking all my attention, as my eyes kept drifting over to the pond behind him. I asked Kevin if he fished, and he said, "Yes, but there aren't any fish in there yet. I just dug that pond." I thought, *Whaaa! Who digs his own pond?* This dude was the definition of a man's man, a He-Man.

As I inspected his golf cart, I noticed that part of the metal had corroded away. I pointed it out, expecting him to maybe take two hundred dollars off the price. He didn't. He instead responded with, "Let's take it down to the shed and I'll fix it." A couple of minutes later, we walked into a large shed, where Kevin grabbed his welding mask and began to solder a new metal frame onto the cart. He said, "I have a welder for fun projects." I wondered, *Who has a welding gun for fun?* Kevin the He-Man does!

He fixed the cart, I paid him for it, and began to load it onto the trailer. But I had a problem. The trailer wouldn't shut. It was too small for the golf cart. I was frustrated. I had rented a trailer, driven an hour, and spent the past hour watching He-Man weld metal. Now I wouldn't be able to take the golf cart with me. *Seriously?*

Kevin noticed my problem and said, "Don't worry. You can just tie the cart down on the trailer and it will be fine." He pulled out some rope from his shed and handed it to me. *Perfect,* I thought.

I then realized I wasn't confident I could tie a knot that wouldn't come undone. I was never a Boy Scout, so the only knot I was familiar with was the one I use to tie my shoes. I knew that wasn't going to get the job done.

I tried to play it cool, asking Kevin, "So, what kind of knot would you tie?" He said, "I would do a bowline knot." I should have known He-Man was an expert on knots and which would be best in this situation.

I, unfortunately, had no idea what a bowline knot was or how to tie one. I debated whether to ask for help or just tie something I hoped might hold. Asking for help might lead Kevin to detect I wasn't half the man he was (okay, I wasn't one-fourteenth the man he was), but if I tied a lame knot, I would have a golf cart flying off my trailer at seventy miles per hour on the highway. There was quite a bit at stake.

Let me take a minute to explain why I share this story.

There is a common phrase used when a couple gets married called "tying the knot." The progression usually goes like this: you meet, you investigate everything about the person on social media as though you're a CSI agent inspecting a crime scene, you date, and you get married (a.k.a. tie the knot).

Tragically, somewhere between 40 and 50 percent of marriages unravel in divorce.[1] Two people who fell in love and vowed "till death do us part" in front of God, family, and friends are later signing divorce papers that declare, "I don't want you in my life anymore." The knot doesn't last. It's tragic because divorce is always painful. Perhaps you've been through it, or your parents have, and you know the pain. Divorce tears two lives apart. There's heartbreak and anger and guilt. There's having to choose who gets to keep the furniture, the dog, the friends, the church. There's having to start all over and figure out a whole different future. And there's all kinds of other people who are collateral damage of this relational explosion.

How could this happen? Clearly, something was wrong with the knot they chose or how they tied it.

Tying a Knot That Lasts

Freaking out about marrying the wrong person, ending up divorced, or forever being single are widespread concerns among people.[2] (I understand—getting married is a big decision and should be a life-long commitment.) Due to those fears, young adults today wait until later in life to get married and often live together before marriage in hopes of minimizing their odds of divorce. Sadly, this is *not* a solution to the problem, and it may even increase the chances your love life will be a romantic tragedy.[3]

Because dating is a relatively new invention, the Bible doesn't address it directly—just as it doesn't directly address Instagram, airplanes, television, avocado toast, or anything else that was not around two thousand years ago.

It *does* have plenty to say about marriage, romance, and decision making, which are all related to dating. Through these teachings, God wants to show us how to tie a marriage knot that will last. Jesus says about marriage,

> "A man will leave his father and mother and be united to his wife, and the two will become one flesh." So they are no longer two, but one flesh.

> Therefore what God has joined together, let no
> one separate. (Mark 10:7-9)

He says God wants to tie a knot so tightly in your marriage that no one can separate it. As we'll see, it's all about *when* you tie a knot, the *type* of knot you tie, and the *person* you tie it with.

The Right Time

Dating has been around roughly the same amount of time as the automobile, as they were both invented within the past 150 years.[4] (I like to picture some scientist in the early 1900s, working in a lab with a bunch of test tubes and Bunsen burners, shouting to his assistant, "Eureka! I've done it! I've invented . . . dating!" His assistant looks amazed and asks, "Professor, what will it mean for future generations?" The scientist stares off into the distance and finally says, "I'm not sure exactly, but I do foresee that it will allow for culture to be shaped by something called *The Bachelor*.")

When you think about it, dating and automobiles have several things in common. One is that they both come with significant risks if handled recklessly. More than 38,000 people die each year from car wrecks in the United States.[5] Likewise, few things are more painful for young adults than walking through a "wreck" in one's love life.

But unlike driving, where you have to be at least sixteen years old (for most states) and go through a driver's-education course, there is not a required age or "dater's ed" course you need in order to date.

Do you want to know if you are ready to face the open roads of romance? You may not want to, but I'm still going to tell you. *You're ready to date if you are ready to get married.* You should not be dating if you are not open to getting married, even if the reason you're not ready for marriage is school, your job, your family, or your faith. If marriage is off the table, so is dating.

Wait. Before you decide to use my name as a curse word and throw out this book (or use it for kindling), let me explain.

The reason is because of another thing dating and driving a car have in common. They both exist to take you somewhere. The purpose of a car is to move you from where you are to a different destination. The purpose of dating is to move you to a destination called marriage. If you are not ready to get married, you are using dating for the wrong purpose, which will only put hearts and emotions at risk.

In Proverbs 4:23, Solomon—who wrote the books of Ecclesiastes, Song of Songs, and most of Proverbs—said,

> Above all else, guard your heart,
> for everything you do flows from it.

Guard your heart. If you are casually dating without the destination of marriage in sight, you are *not* protecting your heart; you are confusing it. Dating should be a path toward a promise of a lifelong pursuit.

Don't get on the path until you are ready.

The Right Knot

The first step in tying any knot is deciding what type of knot you are tying. The bowline knot was the answer for keeping my golf cart secure.

When it comes to marriage, there is a type of knot you tie: a covenant. *Covenant* is a word we don't use a ton, but it's an unconditional commitment between two parties that ends only when one of them dies. Biblically, this is what a marriage is. In Romans 7:2, Paul said,

> A married woman is bound by law to her husband while he lives, but if her husband dies she is released from the law of marriage. (ESV)

God's design is for marriage to be a lifelong commitment between one man and one woman. If you are dating someone, make sure you are on the same page about this. Do you both see marriage as a lifelong covenant?

Too often, marriages are formed as a contract instead of a covenant. A contract is a conditional agreement that either party can end at any point. It's like the relationship you have with AT&T or Net-flix. If Verizon can offer you a better price or AT&T stops providing you with good service, the contract is broken, and you're gone.

While most people still include language in their wedding vows like "for better or worse" and "until death do us part," the divorce rate reveals we clearly don't mean it. Many of us mean "until you cheat on me" or "until you become overweight" or "as long as my needs are met." Before you get married, make sure you both know what kind of knot you are tying: a covenant or a contract. If one of you thinks it's a contract, you both need to know that and agree on the exact terms.

Let me be clear: I do not recommend a contract when it comes to marriage. As I said, God's intention is that it's a lifelong covenant.

The Right Person

Perhaps the most daunting and anxiety-provoking aspect of mar-riage is the search for the "right person." How do you know when you've found "the one"? People say things like, "When you know, you know." I have never found that helpful (or supported in Scrip-ture). It makes it sound like you bump into this "right person" and it's immediately obvious and you never waver. I have not found that to be true for most people, and the idea produces anxiety for so many. *When you know, you know? What if I don't know that I know? If I don't know, does that mean this person is a no?*

So, if you don't "know when you know," how can you know you found the one person you are supposed to marry?

Ready?

You can't.

But, but, but, David. I need to know. Sorry, you can't.

But, well, but, David, my grandma told me she knew, and I can know. Nope, you can't.

Yeah, but, c'mon, I mean, David, some people know, right? No. You can't.

You can't *know when you know* that this is the person you are to marry, but you *can* know if you found someone worth considering for marriage.

In case you think I'm crazy, just stay with me. Contrary to popular belief, the Bible doesn't say to look for "the one" or even that there is such thing as "the one." Instead, it says to look for "someone" who has specific biblical character qualities:

- faith and commitment to Jesus as his or her first love[6]
- Christlike character[7]
- support from your other Christian friends[8]
- a biblical perspective of marriage as a covenant[9]
- spiritually and emotionally healthy[10]
- desire to marry[11]

If both you and the person you are dating have these qualities, you have a potential marriage candidate. If not, you don't.

What If There Is Someone Better Out There?

You might think I am making this too simple. You may wonder, *What if I pick this "someone" but there is another someone out there who is even better for me?* Fair question. In fact, this question is often the primary question responsible for one or both people in the relationship having "cold feet," dating with no end in sight, sleepless nights, and full-fledged freaking out.

So, is there someone out there more compatible, more complementary, and more like-minded for you?

My guess is that there is.

Or I would at least say *there is a good chance there is.*

After all, there are more than *7.5 billion people* on the planet.[12] I'm no mathematician, but that is . . . *a lot* of people. There is probably some "someone" who shares your favorite hobbies, movie preferences, sports teams, taste in furniture and hummus, and so on. So maybe in some ways that someone would be a "better match" (whatever that means).

But contrary to the algorithms of dating websites, finding the "best match possible" is *not* the goal. The goal is to find someone who has what God says to look for in a spouse. In fact, finding the best match is not only unnecessary but also not possible. I mean, it's *literally not possible*. You couldn't do it if you wanted to.

Why not? In order to know the best option, you have to know *all* the options. If I am grocery shopping and want to buy the best apple they have, how can I know I've found it? Only after I have looked at every apple can I know I found the best one.

The same is true with dating. To know you have found the best person for you would require examining every potential option available. That means you'd have to evaluate millions (or perhaps even billions) of people, which would require more time than you have left in life.

To speed date for only five minutes with every single adult who is of the opposite sex, who is between the ages of eighteen to thirty-four, who shares your Christian faith, and who lives in the United States would take you at least the next three decades of your life.[13] (Perhaps I *am* a mathematician!)

Finding the best person for you is literally not possible, but finding someone with the qualities God says are best *is*.

Who You Were Made For

In my garage is a stack of work gloves, which includes left-handed and right-handed ones. When it's time to do yard work, I grab one of each type of glove and head outside.

As long as the pair consists of a right and left glove, it doesn't really matter which I choose. The gloves were not specifically made for the other, but they were made for a purpose: they were made to be worn as gloves, not as hats or socks. I know that, because they were made in the image of a hand. Their purpose is woven into how they were made. Whether a single glove has a match or not doesn't keep it from fulfilling its purpose.

Similarly, living out the purpose of your life doesn't require you to find your "match." Just as a glove was made in the image of a hand, you have been made in the image of God. Your purpose is found in living directly in relationship with him and serving him, whether or not you end up doing that with another person made in his image.

In the same way the left-handed gloves in that stack can match with right-handed gloves, you, too, can make it work with just about anyone of the opposite sex. As long as the person shares your commitment to Jesus as Lord and first love of his or her life, everything else is pretty much negotiable.

When Anxiety Is Good

The purpose of this book is to help you not freak out over or be overwhelmed by panic and anxiety. But there are actually times having anxiety in love and romance can be beneficial.

If you are dating someone who doesn't share your faith or doesn't have the character qualities God says to look for in a spouse, your anxious feelings may be God's way of sounding an alarm: *Don't move forward with this person. You should get out now!*

If you are sleeping or living together, your moments of panic about your relationship may come from the fact that you're engaging in behavior you know is wrong. You know in your heart that what you are doing is sin. No wonder you're freaking out!

Entering into marriage on that type of foundation *should* make you anxious. That's your heart shouting at you: *Don't build a marriage like this!* If you're in that situation, you need to stop, confess, and repent together. It's the best chance, perhaps the only chance, you have for building the future marriage you want.

Another possible source of anxiety might be related to red flags you see in the other person. These red flags may make you concerned about whether he or she will be a loving spouse or a caring parent. If your concerns are related to the person's character, your anxiety may be a gift telling you not to move forward.

What If I Never Get Married?

The question "What if I never get married?" is another source of tremendous anxiety for many people. Reading that last sentence may make you think of spending the rest of your life alone, without a spouse, surrounded by a dozen cats, which is enough to make you sick and want to go update your online dating profile. I get it.

Here is the truth: you may never get married. Statistically, though, the odds are in your favor. In America, 85 percent of people end up married by the age of forty[14] and 90 percent by age fifty.[15] So, while it is possible you won't get married, it is highly unlikely.

Rather than living in fear, you can choose to trust God with the future he has for you and do something that will increase your chances of getting (and staying) married. What's the secret, you ask?

Work on becoming the spouse the person you hope to marry is looking for. Or, as author and pastor Andy Stanley put it, become the person that the person you are looking for is looking for.[16] Rather than unproductively worrying about if you will marry a godly person *someday*, you can focus on becoming a godly person *today*. After all, a godly person is going to be looking for a godly person to marry. Not a perfect person, but a godly person. Today work on . . .

- becoming a man or woman of character
- growing in your faith and knowledge of the Bible
- pursuing sexual purity in your relationships and actions
- tackling your debt instead of adding to it
- healing from past hurts
- serving in a ministry or local church

Are you becoming the type of person the person you hope to marry is looking for? If not, start today. If you *are* becoming that person, keep going!

Hand It Over

Remember that golf cart I was trying to figure out how to tie in place? After staring at that rope and trailer, I knew I had to ask Kevin for help. So I handed over my man card and asked him if he could tie the knot to secure the golf cart and protect it from being destroyed. Kevin tied the knot, and I drove away. I made it home, and guess what? The knot stayed tied.

I understood that if I didn't tie a strong knot, it could lead to consequences and damages. It wasn't worth risking it when I knew someone who could tie a knot that would last. I needed to put the rope in *his* hands instead of my own.

And just like with the knot for my golf cart, when it comes to tying a knot that will last in marriage, you have a choice. Are you going to put into God's hands your love life, future marriage, single-ness, and dating relationships? Are you going to let him tie a knot that will last? Or will you risk doing it on your own? If you do it without God's help, you can expect to be anxious. Why? Because there's a lot more at stake than a golf cart: a marriage.

12

The Royal Family

Career Anxiety

I have to admit that I envy the royal family. Now, I know what I am about to say is an oversimplification of what it means to be a royal, but just hear me out. No, it's not that I'm envious they get to live in lavish palaces. No, it's not that they have personal chefs who make them incredible meals. No, it's not that they get to travel to beautiful countries. No, it's not that they're rich.

Well, now that I think about it, I guess I am a little jealous of those things.

But the real reason I envy the royal family is that they never have career anxiety. Growing up, they know exactly what their future career is: being a member of the royal family—well, if they choose to stay royal anyway.

Granted, that is one unusual career and I'm sure it has its downfalls. Once upon a time, I think the king of England used to make laws and lead the army into war, but no more. Today the royal family has no official role in the government, holding positions that are only symbolic.[1] Basically, they're like the United Kingdom's mascots.

It's an odd job to end up in, but what's odder is that you don't pick the job; it picks you. Prince George, Princess Charlotte, and Prince Louis—a.k.a. the tiny royal children of Prince William and Princess Kate—will never have to wonder, *What am I going to do when I grow up?* They know exactly what they are going to do: serve as a member of the royal family. Actually, let me rephrase that: *chillax* as a member of the royal family. Today's to-do list: Sleep in. Appear at an awesome banquet. Eat awesome food. Wave at paparazzi on the walk from awesome banquet to awesome limo. Drink some tea. Go to sleep. Tomorrow's to-do list? Same. How sweet would that be? I know I'm oversimplifying it and looking past the challenges the royals face—like relentless paparazzi and giving up individual freedom.

But my point is that they uniquely have their whole future laid out for them.

Unfortunately, we don't have that luxury.

We are forced to find an answer to the question "What am I supposed to do with my life?" It's more like, "Ahhhh! What am I supposed to do with my life?!?!"

The most common path taken after high school is spending four or five years in college and then training for a specific career. Typically, the junior and senior years of high school are when students apply to colleges and then select what they want to study. That means that by the age of eighteen, before your brain's prefrontal cortex is fully formed,[2] you are supposed to choose what you're going to do for the rest of your life. *Whaaaaa? Who thought that was a good idea?*

Want to guess what it leads to? Yeah, anxiety.

Uncertainty about work is a source of tremendous anxiety before, during, and after college. Understandably so. It's a big deal. You take a shot in the dark choosing a career and then spend more of your waking hours at your job than anywhere else on the planet.

So, is it possible to have peace in knowing you are right where God wants you to be?

Follow Your Passion?

"What do I do with my life?" Society offers a simple solution: "Follow your passion." You may have even heard someone say, "Find what you are passionate about and you will never work a day in your life" (which is the perfect sentence for the coffee mug you have at the job you hate).

Here's something interesting: the phrase "Follow your passion" was virtually nonexistent just a few decades ago. You cannot find it in books before 1980. But by 1990, it appeared about 1.5 million times, and by the mid-2000s, it was used more than 21 million times in printed English books.[3] What happened? Maybe people before 1980 just didn't have passion?

We live post-1980, and we are supposed to follow our passions. To do so, we have to *know* our passions. So, how do we know our passions?

I've heard some suggestions:

- The work doesn't drain you; it energizes you.
- The work comes naturally to you.
- Something in your heart tells you this is what you were made to do.

People say that if the job drains you, challenges you too much, contains conflict, doesn't fulfill you, requires lots of hard work, or leaves you feeling like there's something better out there for you, you must not be following your passion.

But this entire line of thinking has some big problems.

For one, it might as well be ghost chasing. Ghosts don't exist, and I'm pretty sure a job that never feels like work, takes little effort, pays well, and always makes you feel fulfilled doesn't exist either. Looking for it is a waste of time. Your search will never end, and it will leave you perpetually unsettled and anxious.

Following your passion isn't just chasing ghosts; it's also a wild-goose chase. Why? Your passion will change with age, new experiences, and time. You may be passionate about something today that you won't be ten years from now. At different times, I have been passionate about sports, food, and working out. Should I have been a professional athlete? A food critic? A yoga instructor? Do I change my career every time I find a new passion?

"Follow your passion" is flawed advice. It's also unbiblical. The Bible tells us not to follow our passions but to crucify them. Paul wrote,

> Those who belong to Christ Jesus have crucified the
> flesh with its passions and desires. (Galatians 5:24)

You may be tempted to say, "Take it easy, Paul. You are clearly stressed out. Maybe it's because you don't like your day job. If you listened to your heart, maybe that wouldn't be the case."

No, Paul wasn't emotional when he wrote this; he was expressing a truth at the core of what it means to be a Christian. We believe the Bible when it says listening to your heart is dangerous (see Jeremiah 17:9). We have decided not to follow our hearts but to follow Jesus.

Okay, David, but then how do I know what I'm supposed to do for my J-O-B? Thankfully, the Bible tells you specifically what God's will is for your career. Good news: we don't have to be anxious about being in the wrong job.

Hard Work

It may surprise you to learn that God gave us work as a gift:

> The LORD God took the man and put him in the Garden of Eden to work it and take care of it. (Genesis 2:15)

God created paradise for Adam and Eve, placed them in the garden, and gave them (and all mankind) work to do. God established work before sin entered the world, meaning work is a *good* thing. Work is a gift and is where we use our gifts to improve the world. That was the original instruction God gave to mankind: to serve and care for the world around us.

Sadly, after about five minutes in paradise, Adam and Eve disobeyed God, and sin entered the world. As a consequence, work changed forever. God told Adam,

> Since you listened to your wife and ate from
> the tree
> whose fruit I commanded you not to eat,
> the ground is cursed because of you.
> All your life you will struggle to scratch a living
> from it.

> It will grow thorns and thistles for you,
>> though you will eat of its grains.
> By the sweat of your brow
>> will you have food to eat
> until you return to the ground
>> from which you were made.
>> (Genesis 3:17–19, NLT)

Ever since that day, work has been difficult and challenging. So, no matter what job you choose, it will be difficult. Yaaayyyy, awe-sommmmmme!

When people face difficulty in their jobs, they assume they are in the wrong careers. Not necessarily. Work is hard. You can't escape that reality. Accepting it will help you stay calm instead of panicking about where God has you in life.

Work 101

Work is difficult, but it also provides incredible opportunities. We learn in the Bible that it allows us to provide . . .

. . . for ourselves:

> Even when we were with you, we would give you this command: If anyone is not willing to work, let him not eat. For we hear that some among you walk in idleness, not busy at work, but busybodies. Now such persons we command and encourage in the Lord Jesus Christ to do their work quietly and to earn their own living. (2 Thessalonians 3:10–12, ESV)

. . . for our family:

> If anyone does not provide for his relatives, and especially for members of his household, he has

denied the faith and is worse than an unbeliever.
(1 Timothy 5:8, ESV)

. . . for others in need:

> Let the thief no longer steal, but rather let him
> labor, doing honest work with his own hands, so
> that he may have something to share with anyone
> in need. (Ephesians 4:28, ESV)

If your current job doesn't allow you to provide for yourself, your family, and the needs of others, you may be in the wrong one (or you may have a spending problem and are living outside your means). (Let's be real: I know that most of you reading this do not *need* another pair of shoes . . . or that vanilla macchiato you're drinking!)

The Bible also says work is an opportunity to *promote* our faith in Christ. Through our words, actions, and work ethic, we can be "the light of the world" (Matthew 5:14–16). Work gives us opportunities to "make the teaching about God our Savior attractive in every way" (Titus 2:10, NLT). When we start to experience promoting Jesus at work, we realize getting a work promotion is secondary.

When I say "promote," you might think that sounds kind of salesy. To promote something is essentially to advance a cause. Remember the amazing bassinet I mentioned receiving for our first baby? It was life changing! Do you think I told everyone about it? Did I "promote" it to all my friends struggling with babies who couldn't sleep? Yes! That's what I mean by "promote." We bring attention to what we love or—when it's Jesus—to the One who loves us.

Whether you are a teacher, an accountant, investor, real estate agent, data analyst, professional athlete, grocery store clerk, security guard, administrative assistant, CEO, or pelican proctologist, work is an opportunity to *provide* and *promote*. If you can't do both, something is wrong. The problem could be where you work, or it may be *how* you work where you work. My encouragement: stop freaking out about whether you have the right job and start figuring out how you can promote Jesus there. Quit stressing over getting promoted or noticed at work and realize that your work isn't about *you;* your work is the place where you point people to God.

If you decided your job isn't about you and that your main purpose is to make Jesus look great there, wouldn't that reduce your career anxiety?

Meet the Boss

Have you ever had a boss you didn't want to work for? Me too! It demotivates you and stresses you out. The solution is to understand that your boss is not your boss. Check out what Paul wrote to a church full of new Christians trying to figure out how to live for Jesus:

> Whatever you do, work at it with all your heart, as working for the Lord, not for human masters, since you know that you will receive an inheritance from the Lord as a reward. It is the Lord Christ you are serving. (Colossians 3:23-24)

No matter what your job is or who your boss is, you work with all your heart because you are working for Jesus. Your pay may not be awesome, but someday God will be handing out eternal bonuses to those who served him well.

So, wait, David, are you saying it doesn't matter where I work? No, of course it matters. But *how* you work matters to God way more than *where* you work.

Whether you become a barista or banker is not as important as what kind of barista or banker you are. In both cases, God commands that you put your heart into every latte you make or account you manage, as though it is for Jesus himself.

Wouldn't it be great to stop worrying about your job and start being at peace with the reality that God can use you no matter where you work?

Deciding Your Career

Martin Luther was a famous Christian teacher who launched the Protestant Reformation. A man once asked Luther what he should do for a career now that he had become a Christian.

Luther asked, "What do you do now?"

He replied, "I'm a shoemaker. I make shoes."

Luther's response caught the man by surprise. He said, "Make a good shoe and sell it at a fair price."[4]

This guy didn't need to stop making shoes or put little crosses on them to show he was a Christian. Luther told him to make excellent shoes and not take advantage of people. The heart of the message is the same for you and me: wherever God has placed you, work with all your heart.

Don't miss out on your purpose today by being anxious to find the perfect job tomorrow. You have lots of freedom when it comes to selecting a career path. The chance you'll work in the wrong career is not as great as the chance you'll work in the wrong way.

I know. You're thinking, *I'm sure that's true, but I still have to decide on a career!* I get that. Let me give you some questions to evaluate potential career paths or a job change.

What If I Choose the Wrong Career?

As a pastor of a young-adult ministry, I have had many anxious nineteen-year-olds ask me, "What if I choose the wrong career?" I tell them the good news—that although it might feel like it, they are *not* deciding their entire lives.

Whatever you study in college may be what you end up doing for just a season, or maybe even never at all. So hit the pressure-relief valve. There's actually a good chance you *won't* end up locked into your college degree. In a few years, you may not even work in the same career field in which you started. Statistically, only 27 percent of college grads end up in a job that was closely related to their major.[5] On top of that, you will have plenty of time along the way to switch jobs and career paths.

Knowing these facts will alleviate anxiety and give you peace. Work today with all your heart as though working for the Lord. Trust Proverbs 16:9:

> We can make our plans,
> but the LORD determines our steps. (NLT)

God is in control. Your goal should not be to make money or be successful but rather to know God and help others know him. Don't let the fear of not being where *you* want to be professionally rob you of your purpose or peace.

Should I Like My Job?

I hope you love your job and love your coworkers; however, the odds of that happening are kind of unlikely. Work isn't always enjoyable. That's why they have to *pay* you to do it. If they didn't pay you, it would be called a *hobby*. Remember, part of sin's curse is that work will be difficult. No matter your job, there will be days when you don't love it. Instead of getting negative or apathetic, ask God for strength to continue working hard for him.

If you're hating life because almost every workday is full of dread, it could be time to consider how your job factors into that. But make sure it's your job, not just a negative attitude. It may be that you are in a role outside your gifting. Perhaps the demands of your job are beyond what you can handle while still maintaining healthy relationships with God and friends and being plugged into a church. Those are valid reasons to consider if it's time to move on to a different job.

When Do I Switch Jobs?

When considering a job transition, ask yourself why:

- *Are you running from something like a conflict at work?* Running from conflict is not God's will; resolving it is.[6]

- *Are you leaving for more money?* The Bible doesn't prohibit taking a job for more money, but it does warn about the dangers of money serving as the guiding principle for our decisions.[7]
- *Are you considering an opportunity more in line with your gifting?*[8] That might be a very appropriate reason to change jobs.

Whatever the reason for a job transition, it would be worth talking to people who know you and can help you make the decision. The Bible repeatedly warns about making a decision without wise counselors in your life speaking into it.[9] When other believers who love you listen and then provide godly counsel to you, it gives you a calm confidence.

Speaking of the importance of community, if you are considering moving to a new city for work, do you know a good church there? God commands us to be part of and under the leadership of a local church.[10] Few things will shape your future like your friendships. There is no paycheck great enough to cost you relationships with godly men and women.[11] If your life is lacking connection with and encouragement from other believers, it will likely be filled with anxiety.

You Got the Promotion

So . . . back to the royal family. Interestingly, some members of the royal family go to college, others serve in the British military, and others may serve for a season as a diplomat in a foreign nation. But the fact that they are members of the royal family and heirs to the throne overshadows how they might be working or the position they are filling.

If you are a Christian, you are in a similar situation. You are a member of the royal family of God. You are an heir to the throne of thrones of the King of kings. Our jobs and advancing in our careers feels like a big deal, but there is no higher position you could hold than the one you are in *right now*. You already got the promotion! Your position at work can never compare to your position in Christ.

When you embrace those truths and work as though you are serving Christ, knowing that God will reward you, you put yourself in the best position to move forward through the ups and downs of your career with clarity, passion, and peace.

13

The Secret About Santa

Financial Anxiety

To Santa, or not to Santa? I had no idea that was the question. Until around the time my son turned three, my wife and I hadn't really thought about whether we were going to be a Santa Claus–embracing family or not. If you stop and think about it, how weird is it that we promote a myth to our kids that everyone knows is not true?

"Look, kids, here's the deal. There's this old guy who lives on an ice patch at the top of the globe. He's overweight. Let's be honest: he's borderline obese. This fat guy has a bunch of elves. *What's an elf?* Well, I'm not sure of the politically correct way to say this, but I guess they're tiny people with pointy ears and they're really good at making toys. So they work for Santa all year. *What? Do they get paid?* Well, no, I don't think so. No, it's not slave labor. They enjoy working for Santa. I think.

"Anyway, Santa likes little kids, so he goes and breaks into their homes in the middle of the night. Well, that sounds weird. Forget I said that. He puts all the toys for all the kids in all the world on a magical sleigh, and his flying reindeer . . . Yes, I said flying reindeer. They take him all over the world, and this chubby guy slides down kids' chimneys. He gives you kids gifts, and you give him cookies. So, yeah, that's Santa Claus."

Now, I am not knocking Santa. In fact, I am proud to tell you we *are* a Santa Claus–embracing family. We celebrate Santa with our kids and tell them, "There is a secret you will learn about Santa someday." (That's what I like to call "giving yourself an out.")

No matter where you land, it's interesting how widely accepted it is to spread the Santa myth. We get lied to as kids, and then eventually we discover that Santa and the Tooth Fairy and Easter Bunny are just myths we were told, and life moves on.

What if I told you there are other myths we were taught that most people *still* believe? Myths that have more significant consequences on our lives than if we believe in Santa Claus. Myths that are the cause of many people's greatest anxieties. Myths that some people live their whole lives believing. What are they? *Myths about money.* Before we expose them, let's first think about the relationship between anxiety and money.

In Money We Trust

The gross domestic product (or GDP) basically measures how much money a nation makes per year. If you were to rank nations by their GDP, America is not just first; relatively speaking, our GDP is roughly equal to the second place, third place, and fourth place nations combined![1]

Even still, money is a tremendous source of anxiety for the average American and a major reason we are one of the most anxious nations on earth.[2] A recent study found that "more than three in four Americans (77%) report feeling anxious about their financial situation."[3]

We carry fears about paying off student loans, saving for the future, affording rising costs of living, paying for health care, and a thousand other financial challenges. Financial stress and uncertainty often fill us with anxiety.

Wouldn't you assume the richest group of people in the history of the world would *not* worry about money? How do you explain it? Maybe financial anxiety has nothing to do with how much money you have?

Our national motto in America is "In God we trust." Think about that. Our national motto is not "In our jobs we trust" or "In the president we trust" or "In the economy we trust" but "In God we trust."

That's crazy, because all of our financial anxiety reveals that often it's *not* "In God we trust" but rather "In money we trust." What's even crazier is that we print "In God we trust" on our money! How ironic is it that our money—the thing most people trust in more than in God—has "In God we trust" printed on it?

Why are we tempted to trust in money more than in God? Because of the money myths we've been taught to believe. It's about time to expose them for the myths they are.

Myth #1: Money Brings Security

Solomon, the wisest man who ever lived, writes in Proverbs 18:11,

> The wealth of the rich is their fortified city;
> they imagine it a wall too high to scale.

Why are we quick to trust in money instead of God? We buy the myth that money is a source of security. King Solomon says people see their money as though it's a wall of protection around their lives, thinking it can keep them safe from whatever comes their way. But he tells us that people don't realize this protection exists only in their imaginations. Money doesn't really protect you, just as Santa doesn't really bring you presents. (Just don't tell my kids!)

In a moment's notice, the economy could tank, the stock market could crash, or you could lose your job. In an instant, you'd realize that wealth is not the protection you thought. Finding security in your bank account, salary, 401(k), or job will put you on a roller coaster of anxiety. If the amount you have in your bank account or the state of the economy is where you find peace, you won't be likely to find it any more than you will find Santa's flying reindeer.

The apostle Paul taught a similar idea about why trusting in money is such a bad strategy:

> Teach those who are rich in this world not to be
> proud and not to trust in their money, which is so
> unreliable. Their trust should be in God, who richly
> gives us all we need for our enjoyment. (1 Timothy
> 6:17, NLT)

You might read that and assume it doesn't apply to you. You don't feel "rich in this world." But remember, America is the richest nation in the history of the world. And get this: if you earn $25,000 or more a year, you are in the richest 10 percent of the world; if you earn $50,000, you are in the richest 1 percent.[4] So, yes, the phrase "rich in this world" definitely applies to us.

Paul tells rich people (us) "not to trust in their money" because it "is so unreliable." Paul wrote that almost two thousand years ago. Not much has changed; *money is still unreliable.* Our nation's history shows this is still very much the case. In the past seventy-five years, we have gone through twelve different financial recessions,[5] resulting in *billions* of dollars and *millions* of jobs lost. You know this firsthand because you lived through 2020. In the course of a few months, the economy went from record growth and stock-market highs to historic lows and record unemployment. (Thanks, COVID-19.)

Do you see God as the ultimate source of provision in your life, or have you bought into the myth that money is? It's been said that acknowledging we have a problem is the first step to freedom. Perhaps to overcome financial anxiety, we need to admit that we don't trust God to provide. We instead look for security and comfort in money, or anywhere we can find it, while forgetting that God is the only true source of security that will bring peace.

Paul assures us, and Jesus repeatedly teaches us, that God promises to provide for you. He *will* meet your needs, so let peace flow from his promises, not from a paycheck.

Myth #2: Money Brings Happiness

Here's another myth we believe about money: the more you have, the better your life will be. We realize money is not the source of *total* happiness, but having more of it definitely allows us to buy more things. And having more things makes life "more better," right?

Let's see what Jesus says:

> Watch out! Be on your guard against all kinds of greed; life does not consist in an abundance of possessions." (Luke 12:15)

The word *greed* can also be translated "covetousness," which refers to the desire for stuff we don't have. So, Jesus is saying, *Beware of your desire for more stuff, because life is not about how much you have.* Jesus's words are so countercultural and counterintuitive. Watch out for more? But who doesn't want more?

A constant discontent and desire for more is at the heart of so much of our anxiety. We think we need more clothes, more savings, more budget to travel. More, more, more. We see what others have that we don't, and the comparison feeds our anxiety.

Will we listen to Jesus, who tells us we are playing an unwinnable game, as more stuff will not bring lasting joy? A truly great, peaceful life has nothing to do with "things."

A few years ago, a missionary came and spoke to our church staff about what God was doing in Russia. The missionary had lived in Russia for five years and was back in America for a few weeks. During his presentation, someone asked him what had changed the most about America since he'd been gone. Without hesitating, he responded, "The number of self-storage facilities." I wondered, *What is he talking about?* But as I drove home that day, I was amazed at how many storage units I passed.

Turns out he was right. They are everywhere. In fact, there are *twenty-five times* more self-storage units in America than in *all of* Europe. There are about 53,000 storage facilities across the United States. That's more than the number of McDonald's, Starbucks, Walgreens, 7-Elevens, and Pizza Huts *combined*![16]

Let's do the math: We are the richest nation on earth, with so much stuff that we can't store it all in our homes, so our extra stuff gets its own home! And we are one of the most anxious nations on earth. We are one of the most depressed nations on earth.[7] It doesn't seem to add up. So, what's the deal? Maybe Jesus was right, after all: life has nothing to do with how much stuff we have.

Myth #3: I Don't Make Enough

A couple of years back, I went to dinner with a friend and expressed my concerns about paying my bills—for car maintenance, the never-ending expenses of kids, and so on. He asked me, "How much would you need to make a year to never want a raise for the rest of your life?" I thought about it and then answered, "Two hundred thousand dollars." My friend looked across the table and said, "That's the wrong answer." I had felt pretty good about my math, so I was a little hurt and probably looked confused. He said, "David, there is no number that will ever be enough." I immediately knew he was right.

The myth of "I don't make enough" is one King Solomon, that wisest guy ever who was also ridiculously rich, pointed out a long time ago:

> Those who love money will never have enough. How meaningless to think that wealth brings true happiness! The more you have, the more people come to help you spend it. So what good is wealth—except perhaps to watch it slip through your fingers! (Ecclesiastes 5:10-11, NLT)

He wrote those words two or three thousand years ago, and they are just as relevant today. The problem is not how much we make but that we spend everything we make. Spending all our income leads to a cycle of constantly feeling stressed and anxious. We think the solution is to make more money. It's not. And that desire to get just a "little richer" is incredibly dangerous:

> Those who want to get rich fall into temptation and a trap and into many foolish and harmful de-

sires that plunge people into ruin and destruction.
(1 Timothy 6:9)

The desire to be a little richer leads us to always want more. We need to drive a nicer car, own a bigger home, have more clothes, and go on better vacations. We think that desire will go away once we get more, but as Solomon tells us, the more we get, the more the desire will grow.

We never have enough because we spend everything we have. Well, that's not exactly true. We actually spend more than we have—what we don't have yet—through the use of our best friend, the credit card. *You don't have the money now? No problem! We will let you reach into the future and borrow from future you!* The cycle continues and becomes a trap. If we fall into it, the consequences can be devastating:

> The love of money is a root of all kinds of evil. Some people, eager for money, have wandered from the faith and pierced themselves with many griefs. (verse 10)

If I asked, "Do you love money?" you would probably think the same thing I do: *Well, I like it. We are friends with benefits. I don't know that I'd say I'm in love.*

How do you know if you are "in love" with money?

There's an easy answer. What does love make people do? Love makes us do crazy things for the people we're in love with. We stay up late talking, take on new interests, pretend to like sports teams we don't care about, drive long distances, and make all kinds of sacrifices, all in the name of love.

Does that sound anything like your relationship with money? Have you made sacrifices to get more money? Perhaps you worked a second or third job that ran you ragged? Have you made decisions you regret? Maybe gotten stuck in a car lease you couldn't afford, racked up credit card debt through online shopping, or signed an apartment lease that was way above your budget? All of these are recipes for feeling overwhelmed and anxious.

It's really easy to fall into this trap. So, how do you avoid it?

Can I give you a practical idea that can help you avoid the trap of overspending? It may seem annoying, but *you need to get on a budget*. You need a budget that controls where your money goes, includes a plan to get out of debt, and has you spending less than you make. Is this sexy advice? No, but it is important advice if you want to minimize your financial anxiety.

Will that mean you won't be able to buy everything you could buy according to the credit card company? Yes. But your future self will thank you, because future you will have less anxiety about having to paying off debt.

By spending less than you make, reject the myth of "I don't make enough" and the trap that comes with it. You will experience less financial anxiety.

Myth #4: It's My Money

I have a friend who works in private wealth management. Basically, he invests hundreds of millions of dollars for incredibly wealthy people. Every year, he shows them reports on what their money is doing and how much their investments made and provides plans for how to grow their portfolios. If they don't like his ideas, they tell him to change the plan. Although he oversees their money, it is very clearly not his. He is simply the steward, not the owner.

This might sound crazy, but the Bible says that you and I play roles similar to a wealth manager but with *our* money. Except, it turns out, our money is *not* our money. You are not the owner of your money; God is:

> The earth is the LORD's, and everything in it,
> the world, and all who live in it. (Psalm 24:1)

Everything is God's: your car, your house, the Hot Pockets in your freezer. Even *you* are all his. We are called to steward and use everything in line with his wishes. That includes your money. God says you are a steward, or supervisor, of every dollar he gives you.

So, the idea of "It's my money and I can do what I want with it" is another myth. The truth is, it all belongs to God. The more money you have, the more money you are accountable to him for.[8] Seeing ourselves as stewards means we need to:

> Stop assuming, *If I have it in the bank, it's mine to spend.*
> Ask God, "Is this how you would have me spend your money?"

> Stop thinking, *I will save as much money as possible.*
> Ask God, "How much would you have me save? I don't want to trust in money."

> Stop contemplating, *How much do I have to give?*
> Ask God, "How much do you want me to keep?"

The answer to each of those questions may not be crystal clear, but it doesn't have to be. Jesus says how we handle money is an issue of the heart, not a number.[9] A willingness to steward God's money however he would direct reflects that God, not money, has our heart.

Understanding whose money you are stewarding is not only an issue of obedience to God but also crucial to using money in ways that bring peace in this life and eternal rewards in the next.[10]

Myth #5: Get as Much as You Can

For most people, the goal of life is to get as much as you can. Many of us define success in life as though it's a game of Monopoly: accumulate as much money, homes, and investments as you can, and try not to go to jail.

According to the Bible, the goal of life is less like Monopoly and more like Uno (that card game you played with your grandma when you were a kid). As a refresher, the point of Uno is not to see how many cards you can collect but how many you can get rid of.

Tragically, we have financial anxiety because we are playing the wrong game. We've been aiming for the wrong goal.

- You don't need to make a million dollars.
- You don't need to pay for your kids' college.
- You don't need to own a home.
- You don't need to have your student loans already paid off.
- You don't need to keep up with the Joneses. (By the way, the Joneses are in debt.)
- You don't need to have fifty thousand dollars in savings.
- You don't need to retire by age forty so you can go sip mai tais in Mexico.
- You don't need that new Amazon find that your favorite influencer posted on Instagram.

You just need to be faithful to God with whatever money you have today. Don't forget that he promises to meet your needs and will reward every dollar you steward for his kingdom.

Secret Santa

Someday my kids will learn the secret that although Santa isn't real, the magic he represents ultimately points to the wonder of Jesus, whom Christmas is truly all about. Jesus is the ultimate gift and the reason we give each other gifts at the end of December.

Similarly, one day we will all see the secret about money is that how we use it points to what or who we truly treasure, which hopefully is Jesus.

Maybe that's why Jesus closed his teaching on financial anxiety with these words:

June 13th

Has an appointment

☐ Monday   ☒ Wednesday   ☐ Friday
☐ Tuesday   ☐ Thursday   ☐ Saturday

Date _____ Time 10:15am

with ☒ Dr. Hoffman   ☐ Dr. Lepore

Plastic & Reconstructive Surgery Associates, Inc.

900 Welch Road, Ste. 110   Palo Alto, CA 94304   (650) 325-1118
2581 Samaritan Dr., Ste. 102   San Jose, CA 95124   (408) 356-4241

Do not be afraid, little flock, for your Father has been pleased to give you the kingdom. Sell your possessions and give to the poor. Provide purses for yourselves that will not wear out, a treasure in heaven that will never fail, where no thief comes near and no moth destroys. For where your treasure is, there your heart will be also. (Luke 12:32-34)

Little Kids

Insecurity Anxiety

Do you know what it's like not to have an insecure bone in your body? I do. Well, *I* don't personally, but I have little kids, so I get to witness living with absolutely no insecurities. For example, my son, Crew, is so confident you'd think he was a mini Ryan Reynolds. He has zero concern for how he looks. He can walk around with chocolate cake all over his face and it doesn't bother him. (I suspect he may be saving it for later.)

On more than one occasion, Crew has sauntered into our front yard to say hi to the neighbors in only his Spider-Man underwear. He's not embarrassed at all. (His mother and I, on the other hand, are.) He's just excited at the opportunity to tell everyone about the superpowers he gets when wearing the underwear.

He is so confident, and he makes sure everyone knows when he learns something new. He will approach a complete stranger and ask, "Do you want to see me jump?" It's a trick question, because no matter what they say, Crew *is* going to make them watch him jump. He is only four years old, so you have to watch closely to see the one centimeter he gets off the ground. But if you miss it, no problem—he's happy to show you again. For an encore, he will sing the alphabet for you.

There is something so free, unafraid, and secure about children.

As a dad, I'm sad to think that someday my kids' self-confidence will be replaced with self-consciousness. It won't be long before Crew begins to experience *insecurity* about who he is. I know it's coming for him, because it came for me. Eventually, insecurity comes for everyone.

Insecurity and Anxiety

Insecurity is another form of anxiety. In fact, *insecurity* is defined as "uncertainty or anxiety about oneself." At our core, whether we want to admit it or not, we are all anxious about what others think of us.

Have you ever second-guessed your outfit before going on a date? Have you analyzed your figure in the mirror to see if you still have abs after eating that cheeseburger? Have you wondered why you weren't invited to that get-together or why people in the room stopped talking when you walked in? Have you ever been nervous talking to someone or felt uncomfortable in a job interview? Have you scrolled through Instagram and felt "less than" because you're not married, don't drive a nice enough car, or can't afford the luxurious vacations that everyone else can?

My guess is that you could answer yes to most of those questions. If so, welcome to IBNSA—Insecure But Not So Anonymous. We need to be careful because, just like with other forms of anxiety, if we allow insecurity to consume our thoughts, it can take control of our lives.

Insecurity over potential rejection may prevent you from going on a date. Or it may keep you from a promotion at work because you're too afraid of what others will think and so you don't share your ideas. Or you may simply miss out on opportunities and friendships because you're too intimidated to initiate a conversation with certain people. Insecurity about your body may cause a toxic self-image that leads to an eating disorder.

Where do these insecurities come from? The scientific answer is *just about anywhere.* Okay, that might not be scientific. Insecurity can be the result of the family you grew up in, the way you look, the place where you work, your relationship status, the amount in your bank account, or shame from past decisions. Or you might not even know where it came from.

But consider how your life is negatively affected by your battle with insecurity. Your insecurities influence how you see yourself, relate to others, and make decisions.

The good news is that your life does not have to be plagued by insecurity. While the Bible doesn't lay out an overnight cure, it does give us the tools to battle it.

Sticks and Stones

When I was growing up, we were taught to tell the mean kids, "Sticks and stones may break my bones, but words will never hurt me," and my personal favorite, "I'm rubber and you're glue; whatever you say bounces off me and sticks to you." The idea of both is, "No matter what you say, your words cannot hurt me."

While those felt like good comebacks in fourth grade, they were definitely not true. Some of our most painful moments result from things people said to or about us. Those words burrowed into our hearts and formed insecurities we still carry today.

Perhaps you don't like smiling in pictures because people made fun of you when you had braces and you still feel ashamed of your teeth.

Maybe you were a late bloomer and didn't hit puberty until sometime in high school. The embarrassment of being in tenth grade and not having armpit hair lasted well past high school. In fact, maybe you still feel insecure about your masculinity today.

A sibling might have called you stupid or fat. His or her words shaped who you have become. You obtained two master's degrees or work out three or four times a week because somewhere inside you is a scarred eighth grader trying to prove he's not what he was called.

God doesn't want you to be anxious and insecure; he wants you to experience a life full of peace, comfortable in your own skin.

Thankfully, he gives us the tools to battle insecurity.

Ant-Man

The book of Judges contains the stories of the judges God chose to lead his people. A *judge* back then was not like Judge Judy, with a black gown and a gavel. He or she was closer to the nation's warrior and defender. (I will admit that I enjoy imagining Judge Judy leading the armies of Israel into battle.)

If you read the book, the men and women God appointed resemble something like Marvel's Avengers today. These include superstrong Samson, a.k.a. the Hulk (chapters 14–16), Deborah the Wonder Woman (chapters 4–5), and Ehud, who like Hawkeye was a left-handed assassin (chapter 3). God recruited each of those gifted men and women to lead and rescue the nation of Israel.

Why did the nation need saving? Basically, because the people kept sinning against God by worshipping foreign gods or idols. God had told them, "If you worship foreign gods"—which, by the way, were not actually real gods at all—"I will let you have foreign rulers." Despite the warning, people did not listen, and God allowed them to be conquered by foreign nations. Eventually, the Israelites would cry out to God, saying, "We're sorry. We're really, really, really sorry. Like, totally sorry. Please save us!" In response, God would send a judge to deliver them.

In Judges 6, we read of one of these times. Israel had been conquered by the Midianites, who had reduced the citizens of Israel to starvation (see verse 6). The people cry out to God for someone to save them.

God chooses a new judge: Gideon. Gideon is, well . . . let's just say he's not like the other judges. He wouldn't make it on a team of superheroes. On the Avengers, he'd probably be Ant-Man. Gideon has no superpowers, but he does have . . . a ton of insecurity. (I picture Gideon wearing an ugly, drab brown superhero outfit with a droopy "I" on the chest. When people ask him, "What's the 'I' stand for?" he is too self-conscious to answer, but some knowledgeable bystander whispers, "It's for insecurity. He's super-insecure.") (To be clear, none of that is in the Bible. We just know Gideon had a lot of insecurity, and I have an active imagination.)

We're told God comes to Gideon when he "was threshing wheat at the bottom of a winepress to hide the grain from the Midianites" (verse 11, NLT).

Remember that time you were "threshing wheat at the bottom of a winepress"? No, you never have? Oh, me neither. So, what in the world does that mean?

A winepress was basically a deep hole in the ground you would put grapes in and then go into to stand on them to get the juice to make wine. Threshing wheat was what you did to make bread from grains. People threshed wheat in open spaces because a good amount of room was required and the breeze helped carry away the chaff. There was *not* much room (or breeze) in a winepress. It was maybe the worst place to thresh wheat, but at least it was out of sight.

While hiding in the pit, Gideon hears a voice and realizes he is not alone:

> The angel of the LORD appeared to him and said, "Mighty hero, the LORD is with you!" (verse 12, NLT)

Wait a second. Mighty hero? He's terrified and at the bottom of a pit plucking wheat kernels. God then says to Gideon,

> Go with the strength you have, and rescue Israel from the Midianites. I am sending you! (verse 14, NLT)

What Gideon does next is what we all do at times: he begins to point out why he doesn't have what it takes:

> How can I rescue Israel? My clan is the weakest in the whole tribe of Manasseh, and I am the least in my entire family! (verse 15, NLT)

Ever felt insecure about yourself or your family? So did Gideon. He was totally insecure. But God saw more in Gideon than Gideon saw in himself.

Ready for something crazy? God sees more in *you* than you see in you, and what God says about you is what's most true about you. If you can learn to embrace who God says you are, you will have less insecurity.

Old Dog, New Name

A friend of mine adopted a nine-year-old bulldog from neighbors who were moving and couldn't take the dog with them. The bulldog had been named Sophie for nine years. My friend and his wife decided they wanted to change her name to Fran.

In dog years, a nine-year-old bulldog is sixty-three! So, this would be like someone deciding to change their name about the time they can legally retire.

But out with Sophie, in with Fran! They were now the dog owners and they had the right to change Sophie's—whoops, I mean Fran's—name. That's always true, isn't it? Only a couple of people have the right to name something: the maker or owner.

If Nike makes a pair of shoes and names them Nike Air Max Trainers, Adidas does not have the right to change the name, because Adidas is not the maker.

If you want to change my son's name from Crew to Spider-Man Underwear Boy, you cannot do that. He would love it, but you are not his maker or owner and so you don't have the authority.

Only the maker or owner has naming rights. For Christians, God is both those things. He made you. He owns you, because he purchased you through Christ's work on the cross. What he says about you is the truest thing about you and what matters *most* about you.

Replacing Labels

The labels you embrace will shape how you see yourself and your insecurities. By labels I mean words like *smart, beautiful, handsome, fun, outgoing, stylish, creative, athletic, dumb, ugly, lazy, overweight, boring,* and *annoying.*

When you embrace labels based on what *you* think about you or what *other people* think about you, you are putting yourself on a roller coaster of insecurity.

Perhaps people have always called you smart, so you think of yourself as smart. But are you actually that smart? Sometimes you wonder. Maybe you've just been surrounded by people who are not smart? I mean, really dumb people think of someone of average intelligence as a genius, right?

Or it could be you find your identity in being athletic. But are you really athletic, or just surrounded by unathletic people? And what will your identity be when you get older and aren't so athletic anymore?

Do you see how basing your identity on others' opinions or descriptions or on how you compare to those around you will always lead to insecurity?

That's why you need to learn to embrace who *God* says you are. If you do that, you will form an identity anchored in truth. Your God-given, true identity will not bring insecurity. In fact, it will kill it.

What are some of the things God says about you?

- You are loved.
- You were created on purpose for a purpose.
- Through Christ you are forgiven, righteous, and holy.
- You are a child of God.

Fighting insecurity involves embracing who God says you are in a world that says:

- You are how much you make.
- You are how you look.
- You are the job you have.
- You are your relationship status.
- You are what other people think about you.

Those are lies, built on temporary factors that don't even matter in the grand scheme of things. Just as it was for Gideon, what is most true about you is what God says about you.

Living Legend

About ten years ago, a group of friends and I got to sit down with a pastor named Chuck Swindoll. Chuck is a living legend in terms of influence for Christ. He has written tons of books, has been listened to around the world, and was even named among the top twelve most influential preachers of the past fifty years by *Christianity Today*.[1]

At the time we met, he had been in ministry for more than five decades, and he shared with us a list of ten things he had learned. He said something that day I will never forget:

> Know who you are, be who you are, and like who you are.

He explained that people tragically spend so much of their lives unaware of how they're wired or gifted (not knowing who they are), trying to be someone other than who God made them to be (not being who they are), and depressed over all the ways they wish they were different (not liking who they are).

The older I get, the more I see how true this is. Part of combating insecurity anxiety is embracing who God made you. I think that statement from Swindoll hit me because I knew I was often trying to preach like someone else, lead like someone else, and be someone other than who God made me to be. I realized that whatever God wanted to do with my life wouldn't happen unless I stopped trying to be someone else and started being okay with being me.

Know who you are, be who you are, and like who you are. In the end, that *is* who you are, and if God is going to use you, it will involve you being you, not trying to be someone else.

Fearfully Made

In Psalm 139, King David wrote,

> You created my inmost being;
>> you knit me together in my mother's womb.
> I praise you because I am fearfully and wonderfully
>> made;
>> your works are wonderful,
>> I know that full well. (verses 13-14)

God your Maker says you are fearfully and wonderfully made. "Wonderfully made" is pretty straightforward: your design is amazing.

But what does "fearfully made" mean? It's *not* describing your anxiety or the reason you have some phobias. The word translated "fearfully" means causing "reverence"[2] or "stand in awe."[3] It's like when you see something so well made that you think, *Wow! Whoever designed, fashioned, created, or came up with this idea is incredible!* That's what David says is true about you.

I have a friend who drives a Mercedes-Benz. Every time I get in his car, I think, *There's a reason these cars are so expensive.* The doors are heavier. The leather seats feel like they are made from the skin of an exotic animal. The buttons to press down the windows are made of metal instead of plastic. It even seems like the air-conditioning is pumping out higher-quality air. When it comes to cars, the Germans clearly don't make junk.

That's what David is saying about you and me. God doesn't make junk. He fashioned you together in such a wonderful way—from your eye color to your shoe size to whether you are extroverted or introverted to your love of chips and salsa and EDM—that it should make everyone go, *Wow, God is incredible!*

Embrace who God made you. You don't have to be anything other than the man or woman he made you to be. In fact, trying to change you won't change anything; it will only create more insecurity and rob the world of who you truly are.

The Art of Comparison

Like what we see in Gideon, a lot of the insecurity we have is a result of comparison. Remember Gideon's response when God called him a "mighty warrior" and sent him to save his people?

> But Lord . . . how can I rescue Israel? My clan is the weakest in the whole tribe of Manasseh, and I am the least in my entire family! (Judges 6:15, NLT)

He essentially said, "In comparison to other families, mine is the weakest; and in comparison to everyone in my family, I am the lamest." God didn't want Gideon to be insecure (or confident) based on how he compared to others, and he doesn't want that for you, either.

The temptation to compare may be one area where young adults today have it harder than older generations. Our grandparents had to walk barefoot through three miles of snow to get to school. They lived through the Great Depression and may have fought in a world war. Let's acknowledge that all that is probably much worse than what we face. But they were not confronted with the battle of comparison like we are.

Social media, smartphones, and technology have made it easier than ever to compare ourselves to one another. At any time, I can compare myself to friends or total strangers by pulling up the highlight reel of their lives they post on social media. There's always somebody with a nicer car, bigger house, or better job or whose life seems like one vacation after the next. There is always someone who I can compare my life to and something to be insecure about.

The other day, my Apple Watch sent me notifications about the workouts my friends had done that day. Why do I need to know this? So I can feel insecure about how out of shape I am and be guilted into exercising more? Sorry, it didn't work, Apple. You are not fooling me.

If we're not careful, we, like Gideon, can easily allow comparison to feed our insecurities and kill our self-confidence. But self-confidence is not the goal. We need a source of confidence *outside* ourselves. We need our confidence to come from God alone.

It wasn't easy for Gideon, but he got there. He accepted the leadership position God gave him and gathered an army of 32,000 men to fight the Midianites. The problem was, the Midianite army had 120,000 men. Gideon's troops were vastly outnumbered. But God said to Gideon,

> You have too many warriors with you. If I let all of you fight the Midianites, the Israelites will boast to me that they saved themselves by their own strength. (7:2, NLT)

God wanted Gideon's confidence to be based on the size of his God, not the size of his army. He told Gideon to send everyone home except three hundred men. They went from 4-to-1 odds to 400-to-1 odds! God told Gideon he would defeat the Midianites "with the three hundred men" (7:7).

Every man was to take a ram's horn (their version of a trumpet) and a lantern and approach the enemy army's camp at night. Then, at the same moment, they were to blast their horns and throw down their lanterns. It would be like arson and a marching band all at the same time!

Gideon gave the marching orders to his three hundred men, and that night they did as God commanded:

> The LORD caused the warriors in the camp to fight against each other with their swords. Those who were not killed fled. (7:22, NLT)

Disoriented by the noise and the flames around the camp, the army began to attack each other until so few were left that they turned tail and ran.

Without losing a single man, God used Gideon and three hundred men to save the nation. Gideon learned the lesson God wants us all to learn: find your confidence in who he says you are, what he has promised, and what he can do.

Continual Confidence

We have a natural spring underneath our house. It's really bizarre and means I have the only yard on the block that will never have a problem of the grass not being watered, no matter what restrictions the city puts on watering. The spring of water under our house keeps our grass always watered and never thirsty.

We are told in Jeremiah 17 that our confidence should come from God:

> Blessed are those who trust in the LORD
> > and have made the LORD their hope
> > > and confidence.
> They are like trees planted along a riverbank,
> > with roots that reach deep into the water.
> Such trees are not bothered by the heat
> > or worried by long months of drought.
> Their leaves stay green,
> > and they never stop producing fruit.
> (verses 7–8, NLT)

In other words, it's not about how much confidence you have; it's about what gives you confidence. Your confidence needs to come from God alone.

But is *that* where you find your confidence? Or is it in how much you make, your relationship status, the way you look, what other people think about you, or your position at work? If so, you will always be on the roller-coaster ride of insecurity and anxiety instead of having the peace and security God wants you to experience through knowing and trusting him.

Why don't you get off that roller coaster and put your confidence in God—that he made you the way you are, has a plan and purpose for your life, and works everything for good? You will never be lacking. *That* is a constant spring.

Conclusion

A Continual Drift

Practicing Lives of Peace

My wife and I love the ocean, so every couple of years, we try to break away from the concrete jungle of Dallas and head to a beach somewhere.

A while back, we took one of these trips with some family. One day, several of us were out in the ocean in front of our hotel. After about forty-five minutes of throwing a Frisbee back and forth in the water, we decided to head back to shore. That's when we realized the hotel we were in front of was *not* our hotel. If you're an avid beach lover, you probably can guess why. Yep, the ocean current had pushed us several hotels down from where we were staying. We didn't intend to drift away, but we also weren't trying not to.

For the rest of your life, this is how your relationship with anxiety and peace will work. You will be in front of the hotel of peace and tranquility, but if you don't continue swimming against the current of anxiety, you will drift in whatever direction it takes you. When it tries to pull you away from peace, you will need to take steps to move back in God's direction and attack your anxiety with practices that lead to peace:

- Recognize what you are anxious about.
- Realize what root beliefs and values are informing your anxious feelings.

- Remember that God has promised to meet your needs.
- Release your plans and embrace God's plans.
- Request to your heavenly Father all you hope to happen.
- Replace anxious thoughts with what is true, good, and eternal.
- Reveal anything that is contributing to your shame and anxiety.
- Recover from things in your past that add to your anxiety.
- Reframe everything you face with an eternal perspective.
- Resist maxing out your life and missing out.

Sometimes people talk about peace as though it's somewhere we eventually arrive at if we have enough faith. The truth is, the current of anxiety will never stop pushing us away from lives marked by God's peace. If we don't pay close attention, the current will take us to places we never intended to end up.

Remember, Jesus guaranteed this would happen: "In this world you will have trouble" (John 16:33). But he also said in that same verse, "I have told you these things, so that in me you may have peace."

Jesus promises we are going to have troubles come our way. It comes with the territory of living in a broken world. But despite that, he assures us that in him we can have peace.

Anytime you find yourself pulled by the world toward anxiety, you can take the steps outlined in this book to move in the direction of God's peace. This is not a win-it-once-and-for-all kind of battle. Jesus said the battle against anxiety is a day-by-day process:

> Do not worry about tomorrow, for tomorrow will worry about itself. Each day has enough trouble of its own. (Matthew 6:34)

When it comes to your anxiety, take it one day at a time. Fight the current of anxiety you are facing today. Take on tomorrow when you get there. Each day may have trouble of its own, but your heavenly Father loves you and will help you get through each day as it comes.

A few months ago, I was invited to speak to several thousand college students in College Station, Texas. It was for a ministry I had been part of in college that had a deep impact on me, so I said yes without even thinking.

But as the date came closer, I realized I had a problem: I was supposed to speak late Tuesday night in College Station and then speak at another college in Dallas early the following morning. I did the math in my head. If I left College Station by midnight, I could get home and be in bed by 3:30 a.m. That would leave me just enough time to sleep four hours before getting ready to speak again in Dallas. Four hours is not exactly a sufficient amount of sleep when you're speaking in front of hundreds of people.

Over the past twelve years of preaching, I've learned that if I'm too tired to think, I am definitely too tired to preach. If I don't get at least seven hours of sleep the night before, whomever I am speaking to is going to get a soul-crushingly boring version of me.

I was thinking about the poor college students in Dallas who would listen to no-sleep David and wish for death, when something hit me: I have a couple of close friends who own and rent out a small plane for private flights. I picked up the phone and asked them how much it would cost to fly to College Station and back in one night. They knew it was a ministry opportunity, so they told me they would only ask me to cover the cost of the fuel. I couldn't believe it. I thought, *How much could the fuel cost? It's only forty-five minutes each way. It can't be too bad.*

This was a no-brainer!

I asked, "Just out of curiosity, what does the fuel cost for a trip like this?"

"Just twenty-two hundred dollars," they responded.

Just twenty-two hundred dollars? It's only a forty-five-minute flight. Does this plane run on liquid gold?

Then it occurred to me that the plane had eight seats. I could invite friends to join me and we could divide the cost. It would be exactly like splitting the expense of watching a pay-per-view UFC fight! Except instead of sitting in a living room, we'd be forty thousand feet in the air. And instead of getting to watch two guys bludgeon each other, my friends would get to watch me talk for a few minutes. Maybe it wasn't exactly the same, but I still thought the plan could work. It wasn't long until I had six friends who were in on it. Who wouldn't want to fly on a private plane like a rock star?

My plan was to fly down Tuesday night, speak, then fly back to Dallas with plenty of time to get a good night's sleep (that is, more than four hours) before speaking the next morning. Dreams do come true! What could go wrong?

The day finally came. Flying on private planes is not my world, so it definitely felt surreal. My friends were pumped. We arrived at the exclusive airport, walked outside, boarded the plane, and soon took off. You're probably thinking, *Wow, how nice! No lines or crying babies. Sign me up!* There were perks, but I quickly noticed that a couple of things were different than I'd imagined.

First, we were definitely *not* on Air Force One, which is what I had pictured. This plane was old, tiny, cramped, and well, let's just say more than a little concerning.

To make things worse, the pilot was Mark, a friend of mine who helped run my friends' private plane business. This may just be me, but I'd rather not know my pilot, in the same way you wouldn't want your brain surgeon to be your old fraternity buddy nicknamed "Frank the Tank," who everyone thought would never graduate. When your life is in someone else's hands, you want a stranger who you can blindly assume graduated magna cum laude and is calm and collected no matter the situation and won last year's Nobel Peace Prize.

But nope, I was stuck with Mark. Mark is a great friend. I love him, but I knew him too well. He had just left full-time ministry to help run this plane business and often joked about not knowing what he was doing, not to mention—are you ready for it—Mark has only nine fingers! (Which is a story for another time.) That's exactly what you want in a pilot, right? Don't pilots need all ten fingers? There are at least ten buttons to push on their instrument panel!

On top of all this, it was raining and there was a heavy fog. I would be lying if I said I wasn't a little anxious. Okay, a lot anxious. As we flew, my stomach felt queasy from a mixture of anxiety and the feelings of turbulence you experience in a small plane. It felt like we were on a roller coaster with no tracks—completely off the rails.

Looking out the passenger window, all I could see were rain clouds and lightning. Not too comforting, but I figured surely Mark could see, so I looked out the front windshield of the plane. It was all a fog—nothing but clouds and lightning out there too. So, *no one*—not even the pilot—could see *anything*. Big yikes.

My mind raced to the worst-case scenario: *This is it. This is how it ends. I am going to die in a tiny plane at the nine-fingered hands of Mark.* Other thoughts started running through my head, like, *Who is going to walk my daughter down the aisle? Who is going to teach my son how to throw a football? Who is going to provide financially for my family?*

Anxiety has a funny way of making us run to worst-case scenarios.

Want to know the irony of it all? I was traveling by airplane to teach on how to find freedom from anxiety. So, in case you've ever wondered, even people who teach about anxiety have to battle it.

I began to *rehearse* in my mind several of the truths I have covered in this book. Instead of worrying about who was going to provide for my wife and kids if I died, I *remembered*—God has promised to provide for their needs. He is the ultimate provider for all of us (see Philippians 4:19).

I *released* the fear of my desires not happening and *embraced* the truth that no matter what happened, God's desires *would* happen. I prayed, *God, if your will is for us to die on a plane tonight, it's going to happen whether I want it to or not. I don't want that to happen, but your will be done. Help me to trust you.*

Instead of holding on to my fears, I began to bring them as *requests* to God: *God, please give us safe travel tonight and let us experience your peace beyond understanding.*

I *replaced* my what-ifs with the truth: *God is in control and has numbered my days. I won't die one second before he has already planned.*

I *reframed* the situation with an eternal perspective: *If I go to be with the Lord, I will be in paradise and lack nothing. I will be home.*

As I rehearsed these truths over and over, I began to experience peace. The literal storm and turbulence didn't go away, but the turbulence of anxiety in my heart was replaced with peace and a sense of calm within.

Pretty soon we landed. I spoke to a crowd of anxious college students, many of whom had surely been fixating on the what-ifs in their lives, just as I had been on *my* what-ifs.

My friends and I made it back safe and sound that night, though less like rock stars and more like toddlers on the Mad Tea Party ride at Disney World. Ever since, that experience stands out to me as a metaphor for my relationship with anxiety and the choice I have to make when it arises. I don't get to decide when anxiety will hit me, but I *do* have a choice in how I'll respond when it does. The same is true for you.

When anxiety strikes, we must apply the principles God gave us to replace it with his peace.

As we wrap up this book, I want to reiterate a few things I hope you'll remember.

Practice Makes Perfect

I've heard a certain catchphrase since I was a kid playing Little League baseball: "Practice makes perfect." You've probably heard it too. I remember Coach Crabtree repeating it every time we went through hitting drills and practiced fielding.

That "practice makes perfect" motto has been used by every coach I've ever had, no matter the sport. I've heard it over and over, along with "No pain, no gain," "Leave it all on the field," "Defense wins championships," and "Bring your A game." It's as if every coach gets handed a *Clichés of Coaching* handbook and a pair of incredibly tight polyester shorts.

As cliché as it is, "Practice makes perfect" is pretty straightforward and true. You won't move in the direction of perfection without practicing continually. Practice makes perfect, and perfect takes practice.

The Bible says in Isaiah 26:3 that God "will keep in *perfect peace* all who trust in [him], all whose thoughts are fixed on [him]!" (NLT). Perfect peace comes through trusting God and focusing our thoughts on who he is and what he says is true. Just as we cannot expect perfection without practice, moving in the direction of "perfect peace" means continually practicing the principles God says will lead us there.

We tend to think that if we just had enough faith, our fear and anxiety would go away. If we just tried harder, we would no longer find ourselves anxious. But that is not how anything in life works.

Perfect takes practice. It doesn't happen overnight. Give yourself the grace to grow as you fight your anxiety and practice the principles from this book, which God says lead to peace.

Prayer for Peace

Father,

I pray for every person reading this book—for each person battling fear, worry, anxiety, insecurity, depression, and loneliness. I pray that as they read these words, you would remind them that you are not far from them, you haven't forgotten them or abandoned them, you care for them, and you have a plan for their lives. You can use for good even the most painful moments they are experiencing.

I ask that, in whatever they are facing, you would be more real to them than their fear, pain, or anxiety. Please raise their awareness of your goodness, nearness, and presence. Help them to trust in you no matter what they are facing, casting their cares on their heavenly Father who cares for them.

Thank you for giving your Son Jesus's life on the cross to offer us access to peace in this life and perfect peace in eternity.

In Jesus's name, amen.

Freaking Anxious Questions (FAQ)

Is being anxious a sin?

This is a common question but often not a helpful one to focus on, because neither our sin nor our anxiety defines us in God's eyes. So, a better use of time would be to focus on fighting your anxiety, not on whether it is "sin." Fixating on whether or not it is sin can lead to more anxiety rather than focusing your attention on combating it.

Although anxiety can certainly be the result of sin, that's not always the case. Some of us may be more susceptible to anxiety than others. (I'm looking at you if you're an Enneagram 6.) Factors like genetics, personality wiring, brain chemistry, environment, and past experiences can influence someone's likelihood of developing severe anxiety.[1] Even your gender plays a role, with experts telling us that females are twice as likely as males to suffer from extreme anxiety or anxiety disorders between the ages of fifteen and fifty.[2]

What is an anxiety disorder?

According to the field of psychology, anxiety disorders include generalized anxiety disorder (GAD), post-traumatic stress disorder (PTSD), panic disorder (PD), social anxiety disorder (SAD), obsessive compulsive disorder (OCD), and phobia-related disorders.

I won't get into all the specifics, but *anxiety disorder* is a term to describe debilitating, persistent anxiety that often manifests itself *physically* and interferes over a *prolonged period of time* with daily life (social activities, work, school, and relationships). It is not just the *temporary* feelings we all experience of worry, anxiety, and fear.[3]

While we don't see terms like *anxiety disorder* used in Scripture, that doesn't mean people couldn't have suffered from what psychology[4] today would classify as an anxiety disorder. *Anxiety disorder* is simply terminology psychologists use to describe when certain pairings of symptoms appear in someone. But God is not concerned with how you classify your anxiety as much as how to resolve it.

What causes an anxiety disorder? It can be the result of an underlying health condition like hyperthyroidism, hypoglycemia, or vitamin B-12 deficiency. Or it could be the result of a past traumatic event, a genetic predisposition, or a prolonged season of not addressing anxious feelings, which can build up and become so severe that a psychologist may classify it as a disorder.[5]

The symptoms and effects of these disorders may include:

- panic attacks (racing heartbeat, sweating, shaking, shortness of breath, excessive fits of crying, fear of losing control)
- extreme fears or phobias (of crowds, strangers, being alone, the dark, driving, flying, animals, getting tickled by a T. rex)
- ongoing muscle tension or trembling
- inability to relax or take pleasure in hobbies
- startled responses
- excessive sweating and hot or cold flashes
- respiratory symptoms (tight chest or choking feelings)
- gastrointestinal symptoms (nausea, vomiting, abdominal pain, constipation, indigestion, weight loss, irritable bowel syndrome, or acid reflux)
- insomnia, restlessness, fatigue, or other sleep problems[6]

If several of these describe you, I'd recommend telling your church community group or other trusted followers of Christ in your life and then seeking out a physician, psychiatrist, or counselor if that seems to be the right decision for you.

Should I go to counseling?

If you personally are considering counseling, my answer to the question "Can I go see a counselor?" would be yes. In fact, if the counselor is someone trained in therapy and is informed by God's Word, seeing him or her may be tremendously helpful for you as you grow in your faith and work through anxiety.

As I've mentioned, my wife, Calli, is an amazing Christian counselor who helps young people who are struggling with anxiety. Like many counselors, she loves Jesus and through years of training and experience has learned how to recognize patterns of behavior and thinking in her clients to help them work through issues ranging from anxiety to past trauma to self-destructive tendencies and beyond.

In my opinion, there are times that, due to the level of disruption in someone's life or abuse the individual has experienced, seeing a professional is appropriate or even necessary. But I would always seek out a Christian therapist. Doing so will ensure that the two of you share the same perspective and values.

I personally have benefited tremendously from seeing a counselor as a supplement to my growth spiritually and emotionally. However, this didn't replace my involvement with my local church small group, and I wouldn't recommend it do so for you either.

In fact, I would encourage most people, before they do anything else, to get plugged into a small group of other believers at a local church where they live. The best people to help us decide whether to go to counseling or how to make decisions in general are those who really know us, our circumstances, and God's Word. God wants to put people in our lives to encourage us, pray for us, and give us wise biblical counsel.

What about medication?

This can be a sticky one. Many Christians are divided when it comes to both counseling and medication. By now I think we've all realized the struggle is real regarding anxiety. God's Word has practical tools to help us fight against our anxious feelings, but when is it okay to take medication for them?

Anti-depressants and anti-anxiety medications are not *cures* for anxiety, but they can help many find relief. The problem is overuse and abuse of medication that leads to unnecessary dependency. Another issue is that many today use medication as the first line of defense to find a solution, numb pain, ignore emotions, or avoid handling spiritual struggles.

The biggest thing to remember when it comes to medication is that it generally treats the manifestation of your symptoms, not what's *causing* the symptoms. If I have a bad migraine and take Advil, it will treat the pain in my head, but it won't treat the loud electronic dance music I am blasting in my car that causes my migraine. The same is true with anxiety. Medication can help relieve the symptoms, but it can't treat what's causing the symptoms. However, it may help turn down the volume of your anxious thoughts in order for you to better deal with them. Taking medication for anxiety should be done only when you are also addressing the root causes and sources of your anxiety.

Thankfully, the Lord has kindly gifted our world today with medicines intended to help people find healing from pain. Science and medicine are gifts, but just like any gift, we can misuse them. So, remember, God is our ultimate healer and giver of hope, joy, and peace.

Should I take medication?

If you are thinking medication may be right for you, first ask yourself the following questions:

- Am I connected to a *local church body* that can help provide counsel?

- Am I involved in a *community group* where I can share my struggles and be led by believers to find peace and encouragement in God's Word?
- Is there any *unresolved conflict or bitterness* present in my life?
- Are there any *unhealthy stressors or triggers* that I should prayerfully consider changing in my life (like a toxic relationship, excessive alcohol use, lack of physical exercise, an overly demanding job, or specific activities on my plate that feel overwhelming)?
- Have I been devoted to *praying daily, reading God's Word, and serving* others around me?
- Is medication a *good fit* for me personally? How long do I expect to take it, what kind of relief do I hope to gain, and what friends can I openly talk to about my progress? Have I spoken to my primary doctor about whether there might be another health issue involved?

Always remember that God's Word and his church are the first line of defense in the battle for your mind.

If medication is an additional tool your doctor and Christ followers in your small group advise you to consider, reject any feelings of shame you might feel. Let me say that again for the people in the back! *Reject feelings of shame if your doctor and godly people in your life encourage you to take medication.*

Any other pro tips you can share?

While working on this book, I met with multiple counselors, researched extensively, and came across additional suggestions about how to fight against anxiety. (Side note: I highly recommend the Porch ministry or *Views from the Porch* podcasts!) The following are a few other practical coping strategies for dealing with anxiety and depression:

- Spend the first ten minutes of your day in prayer. Mindfulness and meditation trends are just catching up to what the Bible encourages. Talk to God about what's on your mind.
- Eat three well-balanced meals each day and limit sugar, caffeine, and alcohol.
- Get at least eight hours of sleep.
- Move your body. Perhaps try yoga, walking outside, running, biking, or dancing.
- Journal your feelings, and then identify what God's Word has to say about any lies you believe.
- Find a hobby. Consider baking, working out, photography, painting, drawing, reading, writing, blogging, dancing, playing an instrument, swimming, hiking, or biking.
- And, last, please put down your phone. I promise you that social media is not helping your anxiety. Neither is eating your feelings, drinking away your problems, numbing with drugs, looking at pornography, engaging in retail therapy, conducting all-day Netflix binges, or embracing any other unhealthy coping mechanism.

Finding freedom from anxiety is a battle, but never forget that God is in it with you. He is a "Wonderful Counselor" and the "Prince of Peace" (Isaiah 9:6). Be reminded that asking for help is not a weakness and you are not a failure.

When prescribed medication and Christian counseling are used in combination with prayer, daily devotion to God's Word, and personal care from a church community, even those people with anxiety disorders can stop freaking out and be that much closer to God's perfect peace.

Where does psychology fit in?

Our understanding of anxiety, clinical depression, mental health, behavioral issues, and the broader psychological field is something people have formally studied for only the past hundred years.[7] Psychology is unlike the hard sciences of chemistry, physics, and mathematics, which have been around a long time and are based on measurable, consistent, and logical patterns. Social sciences like psychology attempt to apply the scientific method to human thoughts, behavior, and emotions. It's not the same as, say, algebra, where two plus two always equals four; instead, things like anxiety and depression don't always look the same, have the same cause, or require the same treatment.

In other words, every person is different. What works for one person may not work for another. Also, what prevents anxiety for you one day may not the next.

Psychologists do their best to understand, observe, and treat things that are not always visible to the human eye. As I have mentioned, I'm married to a professional in the field of psychology, and I believe it is an incredibly important field. My point is not that psychologists don't know what they are doing but that because there is a lot about psychology we are still learning, we are often making the most *educated guesses* we can.

When it comes to issues like generalized anxiety, medication, panic disorders, anxiety disorders, and sleep disorders—and even *when* to classify something as a disorder—there is some subjectivity, which will lead to a range of expert opinions, none of which is wrong or even something to dismiss. We should embrace psychological findings so long as they don't contradict what God has clearly revealed in his Word.

Discussion Questions

Chapter 1: The Fog of Fear

1. If you were to list the most common moments, ideas, and things that cause you anxious feelings, what would they be?
2. Do you find yourself tempted to deny or dismiss your anxiety rather than embrace it? Why do you think that is the case?
3. What fears lie behind some of the anxiety you most consistently feel? In order to fight anxiety, you have to chase down what you are actually afraid of. Fill in the following to determine what you are anxious about.

   a. I am anxious about _____ because _____.

   b. I am anxious about _____ because _____.

   c. I am anxious about _____ because _____.

Chapter 2: "Check Engine" Lights

1. Using the following prompts, fill out the TRUTH acronym regarding the last time you felt anxious or overwhelmed.

T Trigger: What was it that triggered your anxiety?

R Root Beliefs and Values: What root beliefs and values about God, others, or life in general do you think informed your anxiety?

U Unpleasant Emotion (anxiety, fear, worry): Write down exactly how you felt physically and emotionally.

T Truth from God's Word: What would Scripture say about the root beliefs and values that informed your anxious feelings?

H Helpful Future Response: What would be an alternative action to take, scripture to meditate on, or thing to pray for the next time you have anxious feelings caused by the trigger you listed?

Chapter 3: Dog Moms

1. Reread Matthew 6:25–32. Do you actually believe that God will provide for your needs? If not, why not?
2. What are you afraid God will not provide for you?
3. Do you struggle to see God as a loving and perfect heavenly Father? If so, describe how you actually think of him and what you think he thinks of you.
4. Spend time praying and asking your heavenly Father to correct any ways you fail to see him as who he says he is in Scripture or don't live resting in his promise to provide.

Chapter 4: One Percent Chance

1. What hopes, desires, and dreams do you find most difficult to trust God with?
2. If you were to be brutally honest with God in prayer regarding what you fear happening or not happening in your life, what would you say?

3. Have you ever expressed the previous question to yourself or to God in prayer? Why or why not?

4. Spend time asking God to help you trust him with the hopes, desires, and dreams listed in question 1.

Chapter 5: Gift Registries

1. If a stranger were able to hear all the ways you talk to your heavenly Father in prayer, how often you talk to him, and the things you talk to him about, how would he or she describe your relationship (for example, sporadic, genuine, grateful, seldom)?

2. How many times today did you talk to God through prayer?

3. Do you find it difficult to talk to God about everything in your life, big or small? Why or why not?

4. When you are anxious, is talking to God about your fears and worries a regular response? What fears do you find most difficult to bring to him in prayer rather than ruminate over?

Chapter 6: Subway to Somewhere

1. For each of the following options, circle the one that best describes the thoughts you've had over the past twenty-four hours.

   a. Positive or Negative
   b. Eternal or Temporary
   c. Grateful or Discontent
   d. Full of Fear or Full of Confidence in God
   e. Self-Focused or Others-Focused

2. What anxious "trains of thought" do you most often find yourself traveling on in your mind?

3. What relationships or sources of information, enter-

tainment, or social media fuel toxic thinking in your life?

4. What half truths would you say make up your negative self-talk or fuel feelings of anxiousness in your life?

5. Do you find it difficult to remember and embrace the truth that you don't struggle with control but rather with not having control?

Chapter 7: It's About Perspective

1. Would you describe yourself as a "glass is half-empty" or a "glass is half-full" person? What past experiences, personality traits, family history, and factors do you think have influenced how you see the world?

2. Do you regularly practice gratitude?

3. Do you find it difficult to believe that you can choose to find joy, no matter the circumstances, through your relationship with Christ? How would practicing this on a daily basis change the way you think and feel?

4. What are five things that you are thankful for in your life?

5. If you were able to view your problems, circumstances, fears, and worries through an "eternal filter," how would they seem different?

6. Is trusting that God is in control and using every hardship and trial you experience something you find difficult to believe?

Chapter 8: Hide and Fear

1. Do you find it difficult to open up to other believers about decisions in your past or struggles with sin in your present?

2. Has your experience with church made you feel more or less likely to open up to other Christians in your life? Why or why not?

3. Is there anything you are afraid to reveal to another person—an area where healing may still not fully have happened?

Chapter 9: Cleaning Out the Closet

1. Reflecting on your past, what are the most painful relationships or experiences that affected who you are and how you see life?

2. Do you find it difficult to trust others, believe the best in other people, or be at peace with yourself because of hurts from your past? How so?

3. Have you allowed the "root of bitterness" (Hebrews 12:15, ESV) to begin to grow for anyone in your life? For example:

   a. Is there anyone part of you hopes will fail in some way or you would like to see suffer?

   b. Is there anyone whose name, when it's brought up, makes you angry or resentful?

   c. Is there anyone you'd avoid in public because of something that happened between you?

   d. Is there anyone you are unwilling to let back into your life until he or she apologizes?

   e. Is there anyone you haven't forgiven?

Chapter 10: The Obstacle Course

1. How would you describe the amount of stress you feel right now? What are the areas you are (or are most tempted to be) stretched too thin (for example, work, school, church, friendships, romantic relationships, emotional needs of others)?

2. Do you see your relationship with Christ as another thing to get done, or as rejuvenating to your life?

3. Would those closest to you describe you more as a Martha or a Mary in how you approach life?

Chapter 11: Flipping Golf Carts

1. What are your fears about your future or current romantic relationship?

2. Do you believe what God says about the characteristics to look for in a spouse? If you were to be honest, are there additional criteria on your list? What are those?

3. If you are in a dating relationship, what are the fears you have about your future together?

4. If you are not in a dating relationship but hope to be someday, is the idea of never getting married a fear? If so, describe specifically what anxious feelings the idea brings up.

Chapter 12: The Royal Family

1. What fears or anxious feelings do you have about your current job or career path?

2. Do you find it difficult to separate your identity (who you are) from your career (what you do)? For example, do you think that if you fail at work, then you have failed?

3. What do you believe is the purpose of work?

4. What are the factors that you think should inform a decision to change your career?

Chapter 13: The Secret About Santa

1. Does your relationship with money cause you anxiety? If so, in what ways?

2. What fears about your finances do you most often

feel (for example, getting out of debt, not being able to afford rising costs of living, not making enough to support a family)?

3. What financial myths are you most tempted to believe?

Chapter 14: Little Kids

1. What things about you, your life, or your personality do you feel insecure about?

2. What are the areas of your life where you are most tempted to find your self-worth and value (for example, dating relationships, job, family, looks)?

3. What aspect of "Know who you are, be who you are, and like who you are" do you find most difficult to practice?

Thank You

- Calli, for being the most supportive wife I could imagine. You have shaped (and corrected) how I think about anxiety, fear, and emotions in general. Thank you for the hundreds of hours you allowed for me to work on this. Your constant love, wisdom, strength, advice, and steadiness are gifts I don't deserve.
- Crew and Monroe, for filling my heart with more joy than I deserve or could express. I love being your daddy. Thank you for letting me share stories about you in this book that illustrate the truth of God's Word. If someday you read them and are embarrassed, remember that your mom proofread this entire book. Just saying.
- Mom, for constantly praying for my life. This book and I very literally wouldn't have happened without you. Thank you for constantly supporting me and being the most faithful example I know of reading the Bible and praying.
- Lisa and Charlie, for generously supporting our family in so many ways and helping our lives func-

tion to a point where writing a book could even be possible. Also, thank you for letting me marry your daughter.

- Jonathan Pokluda, for teaching me to teach, lead, write, flip a golf cart, and throw a football (okay, maybe not that last one, but so many other things). Without you, this book doesn't exist. Thank you for years of investing in my life. I love you, brother.

- Alaina Haas, your creative thinking and communication skills have dramatically shaped this book and my ministry. Your passion for meeting people where they are, excellence in all things, and love for Jesus pour out of your life.

- Ramsey Pittman, thank you for reading, editing, and combing through every word written by your undiagnosed but likely dyslexic boss and making it better. Everyone who reads this book can do so only because you made that possible. Thank you for constantly serving me and my family, helping to keep things in order, and being in our lives.

- Carson & Kelsey, Ryan & Jenny, Clay & Meredith, and Graham & Britt, being in community groups these past seven years has transformed our marriage, parenting, and devotion to Jesus. Your support and love while this book was being written was immeasurable. I am humbled to have friends like you.

- Will Bostian, for being the best friend I know or have. Thank you for your constant support. Also, move back to Dallas already, bro.

- Jennie Allen, for taking time to help me articulate and communicate the message of this book. Let's be honest: I didn't come up with this book's title; you and your team did. I left IF:Gathering's offices that afternoon feeling as though Michael Jordan had just given me a lesson in basketball.

- Dr. Gary Barnes, for being my counselor and helping me navigate my emotions and soul. Your wisdom on this book's subject far exceeds mine, so thank you for sharing some of yours with me as I was writing.
- Dr. Steve Lytle, for meeting with me before a single word was written and deepening my grasp on how God's words can work in tandem with counseling. Lastly, thank you for your leadership at Sparrow House Counseling and in my wife's life. I am proud that she is a part of such a special team.
- The Porch Team—Carson, JD, Josiah, Aaron, Allison, Ramsey, Lauren, Laura, Emma, and others—for reading chapters, being constant thought partners, forgiving me as your imperfect leader, battling for me in prayer as I fight through my own anxiety, keeping the Porch running while I was writing, and giving your lives to serve the only name that matters: Jesus. You are changing the world for Christ, and I am so proud to serve with you.
- The Porch Nation, teaching you the past eleven years has been one of the most incredible privileges. I wrote this book for you and every young adult who's ever battled stress, anxiety, and fear. I am praying God will use this book in mighty ways.
- Todd Wagner, for taking a risk twelve years ago and hiring me. Your leadership at Watermark and in my life is one of God's greatest gifts to me.
- Don Gates, for being an incredible agent, supporting me, and helping this journey come into being.
- Vince Antonucci, for helping write every chapter

this book contains. The color, humor, clarity, and changes you added will help drive people further toward Christ, where lasting joy, peace, and the abundant life is found. It was incredible to work with you.

- WaterBrook team—Susan, Johanna, Chelsea, Dave, and others—for believing in me, in this book, and that Jesus is still inviting people to trade their panic for peace. I am humbled to partner with such gifted and passionate people. Thank you for allowing me the opportunity to be on your team.

- Jesus, thank you that your grace and love poured out on the cross was poured into my heart. Ultimately, peace is found only in you. Thank you that you have overcome the world and are coming again soon.

Notes

Introduction: We're All Freaking Out

1. Howard Ashman and Alan Menken, "Part of Your World," *The Little Mermaid: Original Walt Disney Records Soundtrack,* Walt Disney, 1989.

2. Bill Klein, "Merimna," Greek Thoughts, Study Light, www.studylight.org/language-studies/greek-thoughts .html?article=35.

3. "Facts and Statistics," Anxiety and Depression Association of America, https://adaa.org/about-adaa/press -room/facts-statistics.

4. "Americans' Overall Level of Anxiety About Health, Safety and Finances Remain High," American Psychiatric Association, May 20, 2019, www.psychiatry.org/ newsroom/news-releases/americans-overall-level-of -anxiety-about-health-safety-and-finances-remain -high.

5. "Americans' Overall Level of Anxiety."

6. Sue Shellenbarger, "The Most Anxious Generation Goes to Work," *Wall Street Journal,* May 9, 2019, www .wsj.com/articles/the-most-anxious-generation-goes-to -work-11557418951.

7. Hilary Brueck, "Depression Among Gen Z Is

Skyrocketing—A Troubling Mental-Health Trend That Could Affect the Rest of Their Lives," *Business Insider,* March 21, 2019, www.businessinsider.com/depression -rates-by-age-young-people-2019-3.

8. Ashleigh Garrison, "Antianxiety Drugs—Often More Deadly Than Opioids—Are Fueling the Next Drug Crisis in US," Modern Medicine, CNBC, August 3, 2018, www.cnbc.com/2018/08/02/antianxiety-drugs -fuel-the-next-deadly-drug-crisis-in-us.html.

9. "America's State of Mind Report," Express Scripts, April 16, 2020, www.express-scripts.com/corporate/ americas-state-of-mind-report.

10. Robert L. Leahy, PhD, "How Big a Problem Is Anxiety?," *Psychology Today,* April 30, 2008, www.psychologytoday.com/us/blog/anxiety-files/ 200804/how-big-problem-is-anxiety.

11. Edmund J. Bourne, *The Anxiety and Phobia Workbook* (Oakland, CA: New Harbinger, 2010), 1.

12. Jenna Goudreau, "Why We Need to Take 20-Somethings Seriously," *Forbes,* April 24, 2012, www .forbes.com/sites/jennagoudreau/2012/04/24/why-we -need-to-take-20-somethings-seriously/?sh= 39ee08894a58.

13. "Historical Marital Status Tables," United States Census Bureau, December 2020, www.census.gov/data/ tables/time-series/demo/families/marital.html.

14. "Only One-Third of Young Adults Feels Cared for by Others," Barna, October 15, 2019, www.barna.com/ research/global-connection-isolation.

Chapter 2: "Check Engine" Lights

1. Carolyn Mahaney and Nicole Whitacre, *True Feelings: God's Gracious and Glorious Purpose for Our Emotions* (Wheaton, IL: Crossway, 2017), 46.

2. Eugene A. Nida and Johannes P. Louw, eds., *Greek-*

English Lexicon of the New Testament: Based on Semantic Domains (New York: United Bible Societies, 1988), s.v. "abide," introduction, paragraph 4.

3. Dr. Chris Thurman, *The Lies We Believe: Renew Your Mind and Transform Your Life* (Nashville: Thomas Nelson, 2019), 14–17.

Chapter 3: Dog Moms

1. John MacArthur, *The MacArthur New Testament Commentary: Matthew 1–7* (Chicago: Moody Press, 1985), 424.

2. "The Raincoats," *Seinfeld,* directed by Tom Cherones (Beverly Hills, CA: Castle Rock Entertainment, 1994).

3. Bill Mounce, "What Does a 'Little Faith' Have to Do with a Mustard Seed? (Matt 17:20)," September 28, 2014, *Monday with Mounce* (blog), Bill Mounce, www.billmounce.com/monday-with-mounce/what-does-E2%80%9Clittle-faith%E2%80%9D-have-do-with-mustard-seed-matt-17-20.

Chapter 4: One Percent Chance

1. William D. Mounce, ed., with Rick D. Bennett Jr., *Mounce Concise Greek-English Dictionary of the New Testament,* s.v. "basileia," www.billmounce.com/greek-dictionary/basileia.

Chapter 5: Gift Registries

1. Sallust, *The War with Catiline,* 55.5, in *The War with Catiline, The War with Jugurtha,* trans. J. C. Rolfe, rev. John T. Ramsey (Cambridge, MA: Harvard University Press, 2013), 133.

2. See 2 Timothy 4:13 (Paul writes to a friend asking him to please bring him a coat); Galatians 4:15; 6:11.

3. See Philippians 1:20.

4. See 2 Corinthians 11:24.

5. See 2 Corinthians 11:25–27.

6. Peter V. Deison, *The Priority of Knowing God* (Grand Rapids, MI: Discovery House, 1990), 56, https://bible .org/illustration/philippians-46-7.

7. Timothy Keller, *Prayer: Experiencing Awe and Intimacy with God* (New York: Penguin, 2016), 228.

Chapter 6: Subway to Somewhere

1. Jennie Allen, *Get Out of Your Head: Stopping the Spiral of Toxic Thoughts* (Colorado Springs: WaterBrook, 2020), 4.

2. Remez Sasson, "How Many Thoughts Does Your Mind Think in One Hour?" *Success Consciousness,* www .successconsciousness.com/blog/inner-peace/how-many -thoughts-does-your-mind-think-in-one-hour.

3. Julie Hani, "The Neuroscience of Behavior Change," *StartUp Health,* August 8, 2017, https:// healthtransformer.co/the-neuroscience-of-behavior -change-bcb567fa83c1.

Chapter 7: It's About Perspective

1. Olga Rabo, "The 10 Most Used Instagram Filters (According to Iconosquare Study)," *Iconosquare,* June 13, 2018, https://blog.iconosquare.com/top-10-instagram -filters.

2. "Philippians 1:12–14 Commentary," *Precept Austin,* May 19, 2017, www.preceptaustin.org/philippians_112 -17.

3. Alexa Erickson, "The Secret to Happiness Only Takes One Minute a Day," *The Healthy,* September 10, 2018, www.thehealthy.com/mental-health/happiness/ gratitude-journal-happiness.

4. Matthew Henry, adapted from Dr. Melvin Banks, "What Did Matthew Henry Say When a Man Stole

His Wallet?" *Urban Faith,* November 2011, urbanfaith
.com/2011/11/what-did-matt-w-henry-say-when-a
-man-stole-his-wallet.html.

Chapter 9: Cleaning Out the Closet

1. Touraj Ayazi et al., "Association Between Exposure to
   Traumatic Events and Anxiety Disorders in a Post-
   Conflict Setting: A Cross-Sectional Community Study
   in South Sudan," *BMC Psychiatry,* January 10, 2014,
   www.ncbi.nlm.nih.gov/pmc/articles/PMC3893536.
2. Adam Higginbotham, "There Are Still Thousands of
   Tons of Unexploded Bombs in Germany, Left Over
   from World War II," *Smithsonian,* January/February
   2016, www.smithsonianmag.com/history/seventy-years
   -world-war-two-thousands-tons-unexploded-bombs
   -germany-180957680.

Chapter 10: The Obstacle Course

1. Dan Lohrmann, "Do American Technology Workers
   Do Vacations All Wrong?" *Government Technology,* August 17, 2019, www.govtech.com/blogs/lohrmann-on
   -cybersecurity/do-american-tech-workers-do-vacations
   -all-wrong.html.
2. Lydia Saad, "The '40-Hour' Workweek Is Actually
   Longer—by Seven Hours," Gallup, August 29, 2014,
   https://news.gallup.com/poll/175286/hour-workweek
   -actually-longer-seven-hours.aspx.
3. Matt McMillen and Health.com, "Working Long
   Hours Doubles Depression Odds," *CNN,* January 26,
   2012, www.cnn.com/2012/01/25/health/working
   -overtime-doubles-depression/index.html.
4. Mark Abadi, "11 American Work Habits Other Countries Avoid at All Costs," *Business Insider,* March 8,
   2018, www.businessinsider.com/unhealthy-american

-work-habits-2017-11#they-hardly-ever-go-on
-vacation-2 and https://20somethingfinance.com/
american-hours-worked-productivity-vacation.

5. Daniel H. Pink, quoted in Phyllis Korkki, "Working at Making the Most of Your Vacation," *New York Times*, August 13, 2011, www.nytimes.com/2011/08/14/jobs/14work.html.

6. "What Is Stress?" American Institute of Stress, www.stress.org/what-is-stress.

7. Wes Comer, "Death by Distraction," *Apostolic Witness*, April 14, 2016, http://apostolicwitness.com/2016/04/death-by-distraction.

Chapter 11: Flipping Golf Carts

1. "Marriage and Divorce," American Psychological Association, www.apa.org/topics/divorce-child-custody.

2. Brittany Wong, "The 6 Relationship Problems Millennials Bring Up the Most in Therapy," *HuffPost*, January 11, 2018, www.huffpost.com/entry/millennials-most-common-relationship-problems_n_5a56581ce4b0a300f905371f.

3. "Cohabitation, Marriage, Divorce, and Remarriage in the United States," Vital and Health Statistics, Centers for Disease Control and Prevention, series 23, no. 22 (July 2002), www.cdc.gov/nchs/data/series/sr_23/sr23_022.pdf; "Marriage and Cohabitation in the United States: A Statistical Portrait Based on Cycle 6 (2002) of the National Survey of Family Growth," Vital and Health Statistics, Centers for Disease Control and Prevention, series 23, no. 28 (February 2010), www.cdc.gov/nchs/data/series/sr_23/sr23_028.pdf; Catherine L. Cohan and Stacey Kleinbaum, "Toward a Greater Understanding of the Cohabitation Effect: Premarital Cohabitation and Marital Communication," *Journal of*

Marriage and Family 64, no. 1 (March 2004): 180–192; Scott M. Stanley, Galena Kline Rhoades, and Howard J. Markman, "Sliding Versus Deciding: Inertia and the Premarital Cohabitation Effect," *Family Relations* 55, no. 4 (October 2006): 499–509.

4. "Automobile History," *History,* August 21, 2018, www .history.com/topics/inventions/automobiles; Larry Getlen, "The Fascinating History of How Courtship Became 'Dating,'" *New York Post,* May 15, 2016, https:// nypost.com/2016/05/15/the-fascinating-history-of -how-courtship-became-dating.

5. "Annual Global Road Crash Statistics," Association for Safe International Road Travel, www.asirt.org/safe -travel/road-safety-facts.

6. See Matthew 22:37; 2 Corinthians 6:14.

7. See Proverbs 31:10; Titus 1:6–9; 1 Peter 3:2–7.

8. See Song of Songs 1:4.

9. See Romans 7:2.

10. See Song of Songs 2:15.

11. See Song of Songs 7:10.

12. Andrew D. Hwang, "7.5 Billion and Counting: How Many Humans Can the Earth Support?," Saving Earth, Encyclopaedia Britannica, www.britannica.com/explore/ savingearth/7-5-billion-and-counting-how-many -humans-can-the-earth-support.

13. There are roughly sixty-six million young adults ages eighteen to thirty-four in the United States, which is around thirty-three million young adults of each gender ("Resident Population of the United States by Sex and Age as of July 1, 2019," www.statista.com/statistics/ 241488/population-of-the-us-by-sex-and-age/). GSS Data Partner shows that 72 percent of people ages eighteen to thirty-four are not married (https:// gssdataexplorer.norc.org/trends/Gender%20&

%20Marriage?measure=posslq), which means there are about twenty-three million young adults of the opposite sex for any given young adult. So even if there are one million possible options of single Christians of the opposite sex between ages twenty and thirty-four (which is an extremely low estimate), if you spend eight hours a day speed dating for five minutes per potential partner, it would take you approximately twenty-eight years to meet all your options.

14. Meg Jay, PhD, *The Defining Decade: Why Your Twenties Matter and How to Make the Most of Them Now* (New York: Hachette, 2021), 70.

15. "Marriage and Divorce," American Psychological Society, www.apa.org/topics/divorce-child-custody.

16. Andy Stanley, *The New Rules for Love, Sex and Dating* (Grand Rapids, MI: Zondervan, 2014), 50.

Chapter 12: The Royal Family

1. "The Queen and Law," www.royal.uk/queen-and-law.

2. Sara B. Johnson, Robert W. Blum, and Jay N. Giedd, "Adolescent Maturity and the Brain: The Promise and Pitfalls of Neuroscience Research in Adolescent Health Policy," *Journal of Adolescent Health* 45, no. 3 (September 1, 2009): 216–221, www.ncbi.nlm.nih.gov/pmc/articles/PMC2892678.

3. Jonathan "JP" Pokluda, *Welcome to Adulting: Navigating Faith, Friendship, Finances, and the Future* (Grand Rapids, MI: Baker, 2018), 60.

4. Tullian Tchividjian, "Our Calling, Our Spheres," *Christianity Today*, July 12, 2010, www.christianitytoday.com/pastors/2010/summer/ourcallingspheres.html.

5. Jaison R. Abel and Richard Deitz, "Agglomeration and Job Matching Among College Graduates," Federal Reserve Bank of New York Staff Report, www.newyorkfed.org/medialibrary/media/research/staff_reports/sr587.pdf, 8.

6. See Hebrews 12:14.

7. See 1 Timothy 6:9–10.

8. See Psalm 139.

9. See Proverbs 15:22.

10. See Hebrews 13:7, 17.

11. See Mark 8:36.

Chapter 13: The Secret About Santa

1. "GDP Ranked by Country 2021," World Population Review, https://worldpopulationreview.com/countries/countries-by-gdp.

2. V. Lance Tarrance, "Despite U.S. Economic Success, Financial Anxiety Remains," *Gallup*, July 12, 2019, https://news.gallup.com/opinion/polling-matters/260570/despite-economic-success-financial-anxiety-remains.aspx.

3. Alexandria White, "77% of Americans Are Anxious About Their Financial Situation—Here's How to Take Control," CNBC, October 30, 2020, www.cnbc.com/select/how-to-take-control-of-your-finances.

4. Richard Stearns, *The Hole in Our Gospel: What Does God Expect of Us? The Answer That Changed My Life and Might Just Change the World* (Nashville: Thomas Nelson, 2019), 215.

5. Dave Roos, "How the US Got Out of 12 Economic Recessions Since World War II," *History*, April 29, 2020, www.history.com/news/us-economic-recessions-timeline.

6. "Self-Storage vs. Subway, MacDonald's, Starbucks, and More," Visually, https://visual.ly/community/Infographics/other/storage-facilities-vs-subway-mcdonald's-starbucks-and-more?utm_source=visually_embed.

7. Deidre McPhillips, "U.S. Among Most Depressed Countries in the World," *US News and World Report*,

September 14, 2016, www.usnews.com/news/best
-countries/articles/2016-09-14/the-10-most-depressed
-countries.

8. See Luke 12:48.
9. See Matthew 6:21.
10. See Matthew 6:20.

Chapter 14: Little Kids

1. Kate Shellnutt, "Tim Keller, John Piper, and Andy
Stanley Among the 12 'Most Effective' Preachers,"
Christianity Today, May 2, 2018, www.christianitytoday
.com/news/2018/may/tim-keller-john-piper-andy
-stanley-most-effective-preachers.html. See also
"Charles R. Swindoll Author Website," Faith Radio,
https://myfaithradio.com/authors/charles-r-swindoll.

2. Robert L. Thomas, *New American Standard Exhaustive
Concordance of the Bible, Hebrew-Aramaic and Greek Dic-
tionaries* (Nashville, TN: Holman Bible Publishers,
1981), s.v. "fearfully," paragraph 3663.

3. John R. Kohlenberger III and William D. Mounce, eds.,
*Kohlenberger/Mounce Concise Hebrew-Aramaic Dictio-
nary,* s.v. "fearfully," paragraph 7513.

Freaking Anxious Questions (FAQ)

1. "Understanding Anxiety and Depression Is the First
Step," Anxiety and Depression Association of America,
https://adaa.org/understanding-anxiety.

2. "Facts," Anxiety and Depression Association of America, https://adaa.org/living-with-anxiety/women/
facts.

3. "Anxiety Disorders," National Institute of Mental
Health, www.nimh.nih.gov/health/topics/anxiety
-disorders/index.shtml.

4. By "psychology," I mean the *Diagnostic and Statistical*

Manual of Mental Disorders (DSM), which is a diagnostic tool used by psychologists.

5. Don Graber, "Anxiety Disorders—Frequently Asked Questions," Focus on the Family, February 1, 2014, www.focusonthefamily.com/get-help/anxiety-disorders-ai-frequently-asked-questions.

6. "Anxiety Disorders," National Institute of Mental Health, www.nimh.nih.gov/health/topics/anxiety-disorders/index.shtml#part_145335.

7. Allan V. Horwitz, "How an Age of Anxiety Became an Age of Depression," *Milbank Quarterly* 88, no. 1 (March 2010): 112–138, www.ncbi.nlm.nih.gov/pmc/articles/PMC2888013.

About the Author

PHOTO © ANN PIPER

DAVID MARVIN is the young adults director at Watermark Community Church. For the last ten years, through his leadership of the Porch—a weekly gathering of young adults in Dallas, Texas, and through satellite locations—he has influenced people around the country. David received his master's degree in biblical studies from Dallas Theological Seminary. He and his wife, Calli, a licensed professional counselor specializing in anxiety for this same age group, live with their two children in Dallas.